D1491396

Leadership with a Servant's Heart: *Leading through Personal Relationships*

Leadership with a Servant's Heart:
Leading through Personal Relationships

Kevin Wayne Johnson

Writing for the Lord
M I N I S T R I E S

Clarksville, Maryland (U.S.A.)

www.writingforthelord.com

Leadership with a Servant's Heart: *Leading through Personal Relationships*

Retail Price: $24.95

©2019 by Kevin Wayne Johnson (1960 -   )

Cover Concept by Kevin Wayne Johnson

Cover Design by Emanuel "Manny" V. Brown

Hanover, PA 17331 (U.S.A.)

443-857-2415

Editing, Proofreading, Formatting, and Typesetting by Fresh Eyes Proofreading & Editing (U.S.A.)

1 (877) 728-9618

www.fresheyesproofreadingandediting.com

Print and E-book distributed throughout the U.S.A., Canada, U.K./Europe, and Australia/New Zealand by INGRAM Book Company. Specific pricing added to include: Brazil, China, Germany, India, Italy, South Korea, Poland, Spain, and Russia

To order, call: 1 (800) 937-8200

Unless otherwise noted, all Scripture references are taken from the King James, New King James, New International, New International Readers, The Message, Amplified, New Living Translation, The Living Bible, or New Century Versions of The Holy Bible.

ISBN: 978-0-9883038-5-0

Library of Congress Catalog Number: 2019908365

Printed in the United States of America

Celebrating
Eighteen Years of
Publishing Excellence

Writing for the Lord Ministries

Other Books by Kevin Wayne Johnson (2001 -):

Principal Author:

Give God the Glory! SERIES

Topic: *FAITH*

Give God the Glory! series, winner of 19 literary awards (2001-2013) with selected books available in the following languages: Swahili, Urdu, Falam, Ngawn, Hungarian, and Georgian. Selected books in this series are available in the following formats as well: E-book, Amazon Kindle, and Audio.

Know God and Do the Will of God Concerning Your Life ©2001
Called to be Light in the Workplace ©2003
Let Your Light So Shine – A Devotional ©2004
The Godly Family Life ©2005
Your Role in Your Family – A Devotional ©2006
Know God and Do the Will of God Concerning Your Life – STUDY GUIDE ©2008
The Power in the Local Church ©2010
Know God and Do the Will of God Concerning Your Life – Revised Edition ©2011 [original publication 2001]
Called to be Light in the Workplace – A WORKBOOK ©2013

Contributing Author:

Topic: *BOOK MARKETING*

No Limits…No Boundaries: Marketing Your Book Around the Globe, with Antonio Crawford (*e-book*) ©2009

Topic: *FAITH*

The Secret: *His Word Impacting Our Lives* ©2007

Topic: *FAMILY*

Blended Families: *An Anthology* ©2006 [winner: Christian Small Publishers Association Book of the Year]

Topic: *FINANCE*

Weekend Wealth Transfer: How Black Churches Move Billions of Dollars out of Black Communities and How to Move it Back ©2017

Topic: *WRITING*

Christian Authors Unite: Changing the Way Writers Write, Publish, and Think, with Antonio Crawford ©2017

Writing is Essential: *Use the Skills You've Got to Get the Job Done* ©2019

Praise for
Leadership with a Servant's Heart

"The contents are well phrased and with the real meaning of a leader. I crown the work a bill of excellence and call upon the book to be published for the interest of making the world a suitable place to live with knowledgeable leaders."

—**Reverend David Ingutia**, National General Secretary,
Men of Respect, Church of God Ministries, Incorporated
Kenya, Africa

"Kevin Johnson is masterful in this work. The personal experiences that he shares and the case studies are inspiring and refreshing. If you desire to be a better leader and to help others maximize their leadership potential, this is a must-read."

—**Reverend Dr. Miki Merritt**, Past Presiding Elder of the
National Association of the Church of God

"An inspiring read with Kevin's personal life experiences and powerful examples from industry leaders. Servant Leadership is the only true form of Leadership, and Kevin emphasizes that point very well. With illustrations and thought-provoking questions at the end of every chapter, you will be on a personal journey of exploring and examining your Leadership style and then improve upon."

—**Raj Kapur, MBA,** Founder & CEO - Options Ahead, Incorporated
Executive Director with The John Maxwell Team,
Non Profit Consultant and a Wealth Coach

"Kevin Wayne Johnson is a servant leader who knows the way and can show you the way to personal growth and compassionate leadership with others. He understands that your success is connected to how you influence, impact, and inspire those around you. Ignite your vision with his teachings and see your world change."

—Carla Andrews

Founder & President/CEO - AppleCore Solutions

Executive Director, Speaker, Coach, and Trainer with The John Maxwell Team

"Kevin Wayne Johnson is fulfilling his life's mission through leadership development to our current and next generation of leaders. In doing so, this book highlights key leadership principles and strategies that will transform your leaders in the church and workplace. I recommend this book as required reading as it will raise our collective levels of awareness as good leaders are needed to make this world a better place."

—Reverend Dr. Jacqueline J. Lewis

Senior Minister, Middle Collegiate Church, New York, NY

"Kevin Johnson clearly targets and beautifully strategizes the wisdom, skills, knowledge, and character needed to ensure the gift of leadership is emphasized and shared with impact and intentionality. By identifying the essential core characteristics, he unfolds the key elements that ultimately build an effective individual and naturally an authentic and effective leader. With a particular focus on the necessity that leaders first serve, and then serve with the necessary heart, it follows that others will see modeled what a leader should be in thought, articulation and visible service."

—P.J. Edmund, Sr. D.D, D.H.L.

Bishop & Senior Pastor - Timbrel Churches International, Inc.

General Overseer - Pneuma Fellowship of Covenant Churches of the Apostolic Faith, Incorporated

"I think Kevin's view's on Leadership will Serve all of its readers in a myriad of ways for years to come. Kevin's coaching, using this book as a vessel, will be

invaluable to many and in particular, my clients who I Serve every day. The substance of this book and the way that it will serve as a guide for others will be an incredible tool for change and growth in our Society and quite frankly, it is long overdue."

—Clay Goldsborough
Vice President, FIRST FINANCIAL GROUP, Bethesda, Maryland

"Kevin Johnson details for the reader that a leader with a servant's heart is one who listens to his people, labours with them, and laughs at and with them."

—Reverend Sherwin E.S.A. Griffith
Castries Wesleyan Holiness Church, Castries, Saint Lucia

"A Great Read! I believe you've captured the key ingredients to create a gourmet meal for anyone who hungers for an exquisite and nutritious meal of leadership!"

—Dr. Robert L. Screen
President & CEO, River Jordan Project, Incorporated, Accokeek, Maryland

"Leadership with a Servant's Heart is a mandatory tool for all leaders. Kevin Wayne Johnson gets to the heart of leadership-empowering others. CEO's, CEO's, Presidents of companies should use this as a training manual for leaders. The questions at the end of each chapter help leaders examine their motives, strengths, and weaknesses. As a former military instructor and business owner, I highly recommend Leadership with a Servant's Heart.*"*

—Cherrilynn Bisbano
Founder/Owner, The Write Proposal & Advisory Council for Author's
Community
East Greenwich, Rhode Island

"It is obvious that Kevin Johnson is a spirit-driven, kind and generous family man, servant of God and leader of men because he has lovingly crafted a book that speaks to those very traits. Quoting Kevin, "leadership is not convenient." Being a leader and taking on a leadership role is a tremendous

responsibility and frequent sacrifice. The characteristic of quality leadership is a gift from God and to whom much is given, much is required. Sharing his personal experiences, Kevin Johnson has put into words the very essence of what it means to operate in your gift and to "inconveniently" give of yourself."

—Joan M. Pratt, CPA,
Comptroller, City of Baltimore, Maryland

"This book certainly packs a punch, it is loaded with solid statistics aligned with scriptural references. Highly recommended for men and women who want to be successful leaders in any field."

—Dr. Reg Morais
Founder, Anoint the World Ministries
Founder & Senior Pastor, Living Faith Community Church Global, Perth, Western Australia

"I commend to you Kevin Johnson's latest book, as he describes not only servant leadership theories, but provides practical applications and examples which connect the dots. As the president of a Christian university, and having served as the head of a 60,000 person federal agency (TSA), and Deputy Director of the FBI under Robert Mueller, with over 35,000 employees, I understand and appreciate the importance of those who lead with a servant's heart. Blessings as you apply Kevin's insights to your life."

—Dr. John S. Pistole
President, Anderson University, Anderson, Indiana

"We are all called to serve. Leaders are called to serve above and beyond all others. Pastor Kevin establishes the connection between relationships and service. Lead yourself to this book and expect to grow."

—Dr. Steve Greene
Publisher and Executive Vice President of Charisma Media Group

Personal Reflections & Acknowledgments

I HAVE BEEN WRITING AND PUBLISHING books since 2001.
As I begin this new journey as a principal and contributing
author with book number fourteen, the beginning of this series of
five69 books on the important topic of *servant leadership,* I will
address multiple leadership principles and strategies that work based
upon documented results from high-achieving individuals or
organizations. I have studied, researched, learned, and applied them all
as well as other principles and strategies during my thirty-four total
years of service as a mid-level and senior-level leader with the federal
government and twenty-plus total years of meaningful experiences
through active ministry work and leadership. This includes positions in
the local church as Senior Pastor; a member of the ministerial
credentials committee within my regional district; Secretary, National
Association of the Church of God Men's Ministry; a certified coach
with Church of God Ministries, Incorporated, as well as the U.S.A.
representative to the Church of God Ministries in Kenya, Africa.

I owe deep gratitude and thanks to Dad and Mom, Ernest and
Adele Johnson, for showing me at an early age the importance of
leadership in the home, church attendance, and having a relationship

with God. Dad, a retired United States Marine, instilled discipline in the life of his eldest son while my mom ultimately directed me toward a fulfilling career with the federal government following my graduation from Virginia Commonwealth University. I am also grateful for my wife, Gail, a dynamic leader in her own right, and our three sons, Kevin, Chris, and Cameron, for allowing me some space to pursue my goals, aspirations, and dreams while raising them from boys to men. I am a better person because of my family and personal relationships.

As you read and study the leadership principles and strategies highlighted in this book, pass them on to the current and next generation of leaders so that together we can make this world a better place.

—Kevin

Contents

As a leader, you attract who you are—not who you want. The best leaders DO NOT lead others through force, intimidation, position, or manipulation. Instead, exchange, persuasion, and respect are the proven principles that create a win-win scenario.

A READER'S GUIDE: 215

"Watch over your heart

with all diligence,

For from it flow

the springs of life."

Proverbs 4:23 (Amplified)

"During my lifetime of learning, I've concluded that a leader must exhibit character, energy, drive, tenacity, and unmatched ethical behavior in every area of one's life. To achieve the desired outcome(s), the leader IS the example which others emulate while at the same time formulate lifelong relationships that impact the next generation in a positive and productive manner."

—Kevin Wayne Johnson

Introduction & Overview

*L*EADERSHIP WITH A SERVANT'S HEART exposes front-line, mid-level, and senior-level leaders of small, medium, and large organizations to practical and proven leadership principles, strategies, facts, and real-time examples. Our readers should begin in high school and college and this includes the well-educated and progressive population of Millennials. Multiple proven lesson plans will enhance personal relationships while increasing performance and productivity.

This book's principal goal is to teach, coach, mentor, and share several aspects of leading others by *valuing* and *caring* for them. While it is true that *"... many will not remember what you say, but most will remember how you make them feel,"* the readers of this book will learn the truth of this emotion and how to effect change in their respective leadership styles. When leaders *value* and *care* for those who they are entrusted to lead, their influence increases exponentially.

Leadership with a Servant's Heart is systematically divided into three parts, three chapters each, for a total of nine chapters emphasizing the core characteristics of a *servant leader* which are *serving, inspiring, and leading:*

Part I - The **KEY** to Servant Leadership: *Serving Others*

Part II - The **GOAL** of Servant Leadership: *Inspiring Others*

Part III - The **RESULT** of Servant Leadership: *Leading Others*

My target audience is adult readers in the Christian and general marketplaces with specific emphasis on two primary groups of readers and learners:

1) *Baby boomers* (born between 1946 and 1964) who are exiting the job market (or have already exited) and are seeking new and innovative opportunities to lead new businesses, people, and organizations and to mentor others into their second careers. This group of 53- to 71-year-olds recognizes that their prior approaches to leadership were not always effective and are open to applying new and innovative strategies.

2) *Generation X* (born between 1965 and 1980) who are transitioning into mid-level and senior-level positions within their respective companies, organizations, and/or churches and who are actively seeking guidance, coaching, mentoring, and training on how to be effective leaders. This group of 37- to 52-year-olds sandwiched between the *baby boomers* and *Millennials* seek to rebuild trust and overcome betrayal that they experienced in their respective workplaces.

Both audiences acknowledge a deficiency in their *servant* leadership acumen and in their reliance upon their faith in God. These two targeted audiences include readers of well-known and established authors on leadership principles and strategies (but not necessarily *servant* leadership) such as Dr. Myles Munroe, Dr. John C. Maxwell, Simon Sinek, Peter Drucker, Zig Ziglar, and Ken Blanchard.

In April 2014, the United States Census reported that there were 76.4 million *baby boomers* living in the United States. Acknowledging this huge population, on June 26, 2016, *The Miami Herald's* newspaper article titled "Baby Boomer's Retirement: The Country's Biggest and

Most Predictable Train Wreck?" by Dan Voorhis, offered both eye-opening and thought-provoking truths about this aging population who are not retiring as their parents did. As referenced in the article, a survey conducted by The Insured Retirement Institute unleashed the following data from a select group of *baby boomers* on why they will continue to work:

- This group needs to keep working because of medical reasons.
- One in five said they are concerned they will not have enough savings to cover basic living expenses.
- Many are lonely and lack purpose.
- Many feel that they still have a lot to offer.
- Given the 'skills gap,' this group's expertise is still needed.

Additionally, for this aging population, based upon a Wichita State University forecast, it was reported that:

- Between 2014 and 2029, the age 65-plus population will grow almost 7 times faster than the overall population from 65,000 to 111,000, and
- By 2029, 20 percent of the population will be 65-plus, up from 13 percent now.

Conversely, in *The Generation X Report*, A Quarterly Research Report from the Longitudinal Study of American Youth, Volume 1, Issue 1, Fall 2011, titled "Active, Balanced and Happy: These Young Americans are Not Bowling Alone," the Generation X achievements, attitudes, and behaviors are explored. For the 'Education and Employment' category, it was reported that:

- This group works hard and many continue to pursue additional education.
- Eighty-six percent work part-time or full-time.
- Forty percent spend 50 or more hours each week working and

commuting.

- Seventy-nine percent of women are in the workforce and 57% worked 40 hours or more hours each week.

- Job satisfaction levels were 7.0 (out of 10.0) with 24% rating their job at 9.0 or 10.0 on the satisfaction scale.

- Thirty-three percent are actively involved in a church or religious group.

- Forty-seven percent read 6-plus book per year.

For both targeted audiences, front-line, middle and senior-level leaders from the *baby boomer* and *Generation X* categories will learn and be encouraged to emphasize *relationships* over productivity by *serving others, inspiring others, and leading others* as their preferred and most effective leadership style.

Foreword

I AM A STUDENT OF LEADERSHIP. Because you are reading these words, I suspect that you may be a student of leadership as well. There have been many powerful, wonderful books written on this important subject. Some would say too many, but I would disagree. We all learn differently, respond to different voices, and have our preferred ways of learning. An article, speech, or book on leadership that moves one person to take massive action will likely not have that sort of impact on everyone.

The author of this book, Kevin Wayne Johnson, and I know each other because of our association with the most influential voice in leadership in a generation. There are many leadership gurus, quantify gurus, and pretend gurus. None can match the depth of understanding and the power of communication and reach of Dr. John C. Maxwell. If there was a Mount Rushmore monument to leaders, there is no doubt that John Maxwell's face would be one of those recognized.

Although he has yet to reach Dr. Maxwell's level of fame, reach, and influence, Kevin has every right to be very proud of the work he's put into this volume. I am certainly honored to contribute my small piece.

There is a paradox in leadership that man has wrestled with for generations. It is the indisputable fact that there is no such thing as a leader without followers. Put another way, the measure of leadership is the impact the leader has on others. If there are no followers or there are followers but no impact, the individual calling himself a leader is delusional.

So what is the paradox? you might ask. It is the other indisputable fact that the foundation of all leaders is self-leadership. A leader who attempts to influence others only by writing or speaking but not by his actions will eventually discover that his hypocrisy undermines the benefits of his words.

If you aspire to develop or grow your leadership ability, you will do well to remember to take this tongue-twister to heart: *"Your walk talks and your talk talks but your walk talks louder than your talk talks."*

As you make your way through this book, you will find real-world examples that bring leadership to life. It is one thing to preach about principles and values. They certainly have their place and we should know that. As you probably know, the best leadership is done by example. This is why Kevin uses so many examples to illustrate the application of leadership in specific circumstances.

At the end of the day, it is not so much how much you know about leadership but how well you practice it. I challenge you to challenge yourself to put leadership into practice in your life, your home life, your work life, your spiritual life, and your social life. It is a bold claim, but I tell you that it will make you a better person and a source of inspiration and value to people in your circle and beyond.

Although I am hardly alone in my respect and admiration for Jack Welch and Vince Lombardi, I took note and I appreciate Kevin's use of these men as leadership role models. Jack Welch, the famous business leader of General Electric, is a fellow Bostonian. I know I am in the majority in appreciating his wisdom and straight talk. I may be in the minority on this one, but I actually like his Boston accent.

Vince Lombardi, the legendary football coach, has influenced leaders far beyond the football field or even the world of sports. Yes, he challenged his followers and was often outwardly harsh in his tone and nature. As you may have already discovered, that rough exterior masked a servant's heart. Listening to the testimony of many of the men who were fortunate enough to be led by Coach Lombardi, it is easy to understand why his influence remains so strong, nearly fifty years after his passing in 1970. On a personal note, I married into the Lombardi family and have had countless opportunities to discuss this man and his leadership legacy.

Utilizing the wisdom and practical results from these two men and many others, this book provides you with a recipe for leading yourself and others to be ready for growth opportunities. It will also expose you to what "leading with a servant's heart" really means especially when you are leading those who are most vulnerable to mistreatment, discrimination, or abuse.

I wish you happy reading and successful leading.

—Ed DeCosta

August 2018

Mr. **Ed DeCosta** is a John Maxwell Team certified senior-level trainer, coach, mentor, speaker, and founder of EDC University; he is also the author of *Ascend* and *Release Your Superhero.*

PART ONE:

the KEY to Servant Leadership: *Serving Others*

"Let each of you look out not only for his own interests, but also for the interests of others."
—Philippians 2:4 (King James Version)

CHAPTER ONE

It's Not About You – It's About Others

"You can get everything in life you want if you will just help other people get what they want!"

—Zig Ziglar (1926 – 2012)
World Renowned Motivational Speaker

"Shall not God search this out? for He knoweth the secrets of the heart."

—Psalm 44:21 (King James Version)

L EADERSHIP IS NOT CONVENIENT. The Scriptures teach *"...and when He had called the people unto Him with His disciples also, He said unto them, Whosoever will come after me, let him deny himself, and take up his cross, and follow me"* (Mark 8:34).

My Journey Towards Leadership

I have been actively working and earning a decent salary since age fourteen. Over a span of forty-three years, I have cleaned the outdoor pool at a mid-sized hotel; served meals as a waiter at fast food and upscale restaurants; validated payroll; processed business and personal checks as a proof operator at major financial institutions; collected delinquent state taxes from businesses as a taxpayer service representative for the Commonwealth of Virginia; sold insurance policies and pieces of artwork; checked in travelers as a front desk clerk at Holiday Inn; worked in retail as a sales clerk at Macy's; served in ministry as a deacon, prayer leader, adjunct professor, associate pastor, and senior pastor; worked as a manager and director of information technology strategic sourcing at two Fortune 1000 companies in New York City; and protected the citizens of the United States of America through my service as a front-line, mid-level, and senior-level leader with several federal government agencies. My longevity in the workplace, in many different industries and diverse locations, has shaped my views and ideas about leadership both good and bad. I value the mentoring and guidance I received from the good leaders. There were many of them. Conversely, I abhor all interactions from the bad leaders. There were many of them as well. I do not remember too much what was said by the bad leaders, but I succinctly remember how they made me feel—even to this day.

Through these varied occupations and employers that span four decades, and in addition, a few short periods of unemployment, I have learned many life-changing lessons based upon my experience, observations, frustrations, joys, collaboration with colleagues, relationships with peers and bosses, and responses to market fluctuations that influenced my job decisions. One of the most valuable lessons that I recall is my in-depth study, reading, observation, and research on the subject of *leadership,* specifically, *servant leadership.* This is a topic first introduced in 1970 by Robert K. Greenleaf. This retired AT&T executive coined the term *servant leadership* to describe the type of leadership missing from organizations. His book *The Power of Servant Leadership* (1998) offers his own insights on the interrelated subjects of serving and leading, wholeness and spirit as a collection of eight essays published from 1977 – 1987. Over the years, I have been fascinated at the volumes of reading material available on this topic, yet surprised at the lacking evidence that these principles and strategies have been put to use. For example, I recently read an article in the *Harvard Business Review* that captures the essence of my experiences in diverse workplaces for over four decades. This article, "Diversity Doesn't Stick Without Inclusion," published on February 1, 2017, by Laura Sherbin and Ripa Rashid, provides an excellent overview of inclusive leaders. This style of leadership is a conglomeration of *six* behaviors:

- Ensuring that team members speak up and are heard
- Making it safe to propose novel ideas
- Empowering team members to make decisions
- Taking advice and implementing feedback
- Giving actionable feedback
- Sharing credit for team success

This insightful and thought-provoking reading acknowledges that when surveyed, the employees who report that their team leader exemplifies at least three of the above-mentioned behaviors, produce the following results in the workplace:

87% say they feel welcome and included in their team, **87%** say they feel free to express their views and opinions, and **74%** say they feel that their ideas are heard and recognized. For respondents who reported that their team leader has **none** of these traits, those percentages dropped to **51%**, **46%** and **37%**, respectively.

"Leadership is about influence, nothing more, nothing less," says leadership expert John C. Maxwell. With this practice in mind, it is worth exploring how leaders must place the needs of *others* before themselves. In doing so, perhaps we can mirror the data above by being more inclusive, valuing others' views and opinions, listening to and recognizing their contributions and gifts to our respective organizations. This is a universal theme that can be applied in our corporations, governments, academia, non-profit organizations, and churches.

The Iceberg Effect

Further evidence supports our need to focus on *others* as a means to develop, train, and retain good leaders.

The Iceberg Effect is a visual portrayal of how and why we judge others based upon our own perceptions. We envision <u>who</u> a person is based upon what we observe on the outside without having insights into their hearts, life experiences, or innermost feelings. Through our misplaced actions or thoughts, we make an unconscious error when a distorted judgment is created. We do not embrace their potential. We cannot 'see' the total person. Thus, we minimize their existence based upon very limited information and prior to establishing a meaningful relationship.

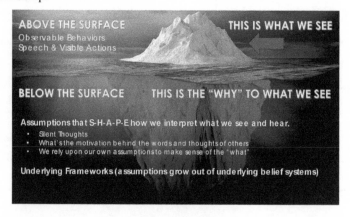

The top portion of the iceberg that is visible for all to 'see,' only represents 20% of its total composition. During our interactions with others, behaviors such as speech, behavior, actions, and mannerisms are all visible. Conversely, 80% of the iceberg is not visible. This is the portion of the iceberg that is under the water. It is a representation of the 'why' to what we do see (20%). As a direct result, we make assumptions that shape how we interpret what we see and hear through silent thoughts and our own lifelong belief systems.

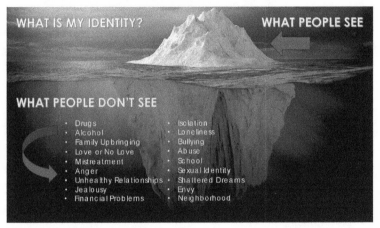

There are many reasons people do not realize their goals, dreams, and aspirations. In part, many of us do not know our identity. Most are a direct result of life situations and circumstances that have been unresolved since childhood. In other instances, there is a correlation with education levels, family relationships, lifestyle, religious affiliation, peers, working conditions, and exposure to love, or lack thereof, over a lifetime.

Leadership with a Servant's Heart challenges leaders to dive deep into a personal relationship with others to understand their *views, values, hurts, habits,* and *hang-ups.* The conversation and dialogue open doors into the 80% of their lives that are contributing factors in limiting their potential to excel. Helping them to transition from mediocre and average into a state of excellence happens during those moments of open discussions. When the eighteen barriers, characteristics, and attributes are addressed in an environment where trust and rapport have been established, then we begin to understand people in a manner where we can help and assist them at their specific area of need. The eighteen barriers are:

- Drug usage
- Alcohol consumption
- Family upbringing (loving vs. tumultuous)
- Love (or not)
- Mistreatment (including bullying)
- Anger
- Unhealthy relationships
- Jealousy
- Financial problems (insurmountable debt)
- Isolation (no friends)
- Loneliness
- Bullying (verbal)
- Abuse (physical and verbal)
- School
- Sexual identity
- Shattered dreams
- Envy (comparing oneself to others)
- Neighborhood

The Golden Rule

"Do to others as you would like them to do to you."

—Luke 6:31 (New Living Translation)

"Treat others the same way you want them to treat you."

—Luke 6:31 (Amplified)

The *Golden Rule* is a universal and self-explanatory principle about personal and public conduct that every person understands and at its core acknowledges as appropriate behavior in all settings. It is a rule (a prescribed guide for conduct or action) that if applied, will serve as an antidote for societal ills and moral deterioration.

In the Book of Luke, the *Golden Rule* is exemplified by Jesus Himself through the writing of Luke. As a physician, Luke writes with the compassion and warmth of a family doctor as he carefully documents the perfect humanity of the Son of Man—Jesus Christ. Luke portrays Jesus as the compassionate Savior of the world, with love for all people, whether rich or poor. He reaches out especially to women, the poor, and the outcast of society. Luke emphasizes the work of the Holy Spirit and the central place of prayer in Jesus' life and ministry. But the resurrection ensures that His purpose will be fulfilled: *"...to seek and to save that which was lost"* (Luke 19:10).

In chapter six of this book, the *Golden Rule* is nestled in the midst of Jesus' work on the Sabbath including Him healing a man with a withered hand. His work is accomplished within the view of the two major religious sects of His time—the Scribes and the Pharisees—whose core beliefs were that no work should be done on the Sabbath. Jesus then selected His twelve disciples and taught them the principles of the Beatitudes and the rules of the Kingdom life. His message resonated with believers and unbelievers in so much as our Kingdom lifestyle will transcend everything that is wrong with our society and this world.

In another one of the gospels, the Book of Matthew, the *Golden Rule* is taught to His disciples and the multitudes during His first public sermon (Matthew chapters 5-7) alongside important topics such as the fulfillment of the law, distinguishing between salt and light, love, the pattern for prayer, missions, fasting, financial management, and false and true teaching, just to name a few. As a tax collector, Matthew is convincing in his writing that Jesus is the promised Messiah of Old Testament prophecy. A major theme of this book is God's rule in the world and in human hearts (*the Kingdom of Heaven* in particular). The strength and royal authority of Jesus are on display in this book of the Bible as He openly demonstrates through His actions that at all times, we must reciprocate kind acts and deeds to *others* as we would expect from them. Take the first steps and become the initiator.

"Here is a simple, rule-of-thumb guide for behavior: Ask yourself what you want people to do for you, then grab the initiative and do it for them. Add up God's Law and Prophets and this is what you get."

—Matthew 7:12 (The Message)

"Do for others what you want them to do for you. This is the teaching of the laws of Moses in a nutshell."

—Matthew 7:12 (The Living Bible)

Yet, we fall short in practice and application of the *Golden Rule.* Why?

Through the centuries, the Bible has been the most widely read of all books ever published; yet as individuals have prompted to read it, perhaps by curiosity, perhaps by spiritual interest, they have often found that it baffles them. In many instances, even those who do not believe that it has any claims on their lives feel, and rightly so, that it is unintelligent to remain in ignorance of the most famous of writings. Still, they along with many sincere believers, all too soon shrink from any serious effort to master the contents of the sacred text. The main reason for not understanding the message of Scripture lies in the failure to see its overall plan and purpose.

Consider these factors that make the Bible different from any other book:

- It was written over a span of 1,500 years (*representation of dispensations of time*).

- It was written by more than 40 individuals (*representation of the multiplicity of people, thoughts, ideas, views, and creativity*).

- Its writers were fishermen, rabbis, kings, philosophers, soldiers, and even a tax collector (*representation of varied professions*).

- Its writers used a variety of literary styles including historical narrative, personal letters, song lyrics, parables, biographies and autobiographies, poetry, and prophecy (*representation of diversity*).

- It was written on three different continents: Africa, Asia, and Europe (*representation of geographic dispersion*).

- It was written in three languages: Greek, Hebrew, and Aramaic (*representation of dissimilar dialects*).

Bible Sales Statistics

Christians take their Bibles everywhere with them…but sometimes they don't. Sometimes the one book collecting dust on the bookshelf is the Bible. Yet this need to own at least one copy of the inspired Word of God drives the Bible to be a top-selling book every year whether it is opened and read or not. More than 2,100 languages have at least one book of the Bible in that language.

Between 1815 and 1975, it was estimated that there could have been 5 billion Bibles printed. In 1995, one version of the Bible, the Good News version that is copyrighted by the Bible Societies, had sold nearly 18 million copies. There's no doubt about it: the Bible is one of the world's best-selling books. It also proves that God's Word is a moneymaker for today's Christian publishers.

- The best-selling and fastest-growing version of the Bible in the United States is the New International Version.

- **82%.** That's the percentage of people who regularly read the Bible who will reach for a King James Version before any other.

- There are more than 168,000 Bibles that are sold or given to others in the United States every day.

- **20 million.** That's the number of Bibles that are sold each year in the United States. That's more than double the amount that was sold annually in the 1950s.

- Gideon's International distributed 59,460,000 Bibles worldwide last year. That's more than 100 Bibles per minute.

- Zondervan, a leading Bible publisher, has more than 350 different versions of the Bible that are in print right now.

- The percentage of Americans who own at least one Bible, whether it was given to them or purchased: **92%.** Two-thirds of owners, regardless of religious affiliation, say that the Bible holds the meaning of life.

- The average American Christian owns nine Bibles and wants to purchase more. For this reason, the Bible is actually excluded from book bestsellers lists because it would always be on top.

- 1,300 translations of the Bible are in new languages.

(**Note 1:** *29 Good Bible Sales Statistics*, by Brandon Gaille, May 23, 2017)

We OWN It –

In the United States, 94.0% of adult Americans own a Bible. No other book comes *remotely* close to that number. Most homes have multiple copies.

Chart 1.

Twenty-two percent of households surveyed own one Bible, twenty-eight percent of households own two Bibles, and twenty-one percent of households own three Bibles. Only three percent of households report that they do not know how many Bibles they own. That's more—*much more*—than *any* other publications.

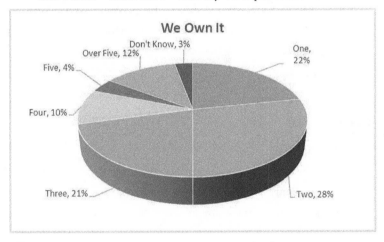

Chart 2.

Beyond that, 47% of American households have *at least three* Bibles (14% own three, 6% own four, 12% own five, and 15% can't recall). We also purchase and give them as gifts regularly. How many Bibles has the average American adult either purchased or had given to them by friends and or relatives?

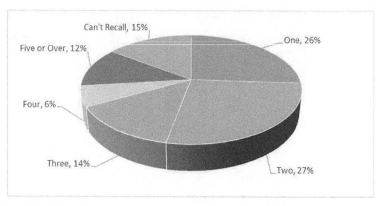

We READ It...Sort of

To a certain degree, the Bible is a regular aspect of American family life. On an individual basis, the 2010 ARG survey found that 52% of adults read the Bible weekly and three-fourths of us read the Bible at least monthly.

Chart 3.

To summarize: 94.0% of Americans own a Bible; 90.0% of us believe it still applies today yet only half of us read it weekly (including in church), and only 29.0% read it weekly outside of church.

(**Note 2**: The Bible *in* America: *What We Believe About the* Most Important Book *in Our History*, by Steve Green and Todd Hillard ©2013, pages 3-9.)

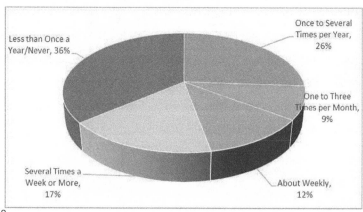

In the spirit of practicing, leading, and living by **The Golden Rule**, it is imperative that we know the overall plan of the Bible. It is one Book, and there are several telling signs that attest to its message of unity:

- From Genesis onward the Bible bears witness to <u>one</u> God.
- The Bible forms <u>one</u> continuous story: the account of God's dealings with the human race.
- The Bible advances the most unlikely predictions concerning the future and then gives the record of their fulfillment at the appropriate time.
- The Bible is a progressive unfolding of truth.
- The Bible presents a <u>single way</u> of access to God.
- From beginning to end the Bible has <u>one</u> great theme: the Person and work of the Lord Jesus Christ.
- The doctrines of the Bible are harmonious even though they were penned by some forty-four writers over more than sixteen centuries.

Our reading and understanding of these truths help us to understand a core tenet of the Bible as recorded in Luke 6:31:- *Do to others as you would like them to do to you* (NLT), as well as Matthew 7:12: *Here is a simple, rule-of-thumb guide for behavior: Ask yourself what you want people to do for you, then grab the initiative and do it for them* (The Message). Lead others in the way that you would like to be led, that is, with respect, value, loyalty, decency, courtesy

> "Down through the years its been ridiculed, burned, refuted, destroyed, but it lives on. It is the anvil that has worn out many hammers. Most books are born, live a few short years, then go the way of all the earth; they're forgotten. But not the Bible."
>
> Billy Graham

and appreciation. Be on one accord. See others as you see yourself. This is how to treat (*serve*) others.

Zig Ziglar – The Ultimate Motivator

Born in 1926 in Coffee County, Alabama, as the tenth of twelve children, Zig's motivational speeches across the globe touched the lives of millions of listeners through his unique and charming personality, body language, and tone. He lived to inspire a generation of followers toward success in life and business through his keynote speeches and multiple books. In doing so, Zig, born into the world as Hilary Hinton Ziglar, amassed a net worth of $15M during his lifetime, in part, because he understood and taught the basic and foundation principles of *helping* and *serving others*.

In his own words, Zig describes his humble beginnings as a means to spend a lifetime of service to others:

Today I'm going to be sharing with you my spiritual journey. Interestingly enough, it started when I was ten days old. I died that day. Ten days earlier the doctor had delivered me to my mother and said, "You have a perfectly healthy baby boy." Ten days later, he laid me on the bed and said to my mother, "He is no more."

My grandmother reached down and picked up this lifeless body. And they said she started talking to me. But you, of course, know that she was not talking to me; she was talking to her heavenly Father. She was pleading for my life. God responded to that prayer, and obviously, I did survive.

As a child, I watched a widowed mother who lost her husband who left her with six children too small to work –there were twelve of us, all told. She lost her daughter just a few days later. And so it was a pretty tough childhood. I watched—I watched my mother's incredible faith.

Now, as a child, every week we were in church. As a matter of fact, Mrs. L.S. Jones from down the street drove an old Dodge. And she would come in front of our house and sound her horn and I can see my mother to this day as she would do two things simultaneously: She would reach over and pick up her navy blue hat and put it on the bun on the back of her head (her long hair was rolled up), and she would reach and get her headpin and in the same motion she would put it all together and say, "Let's go, boys." And I'm telling you, we headed for the car. It never occurred to us to not go. We didn't think we had a choice. And reflecting on it, we didn't have a choice. It was clearly understood: we were going to church.

On Sunday evening we went to what the Baptist call, you know, BYPU in those days. And as boys, we thought BYPU stood for "Buy your preacher's underwear." I mean, that's why we were there. We were in church on Sunday night. We were in prayer meeting on Wednesday night. When the church doors opened, we were there.

On a number of occasions . . . and incidentally, I was baptized when I was twelve years old. I was as lost as a human being could get. I don't know why I was baptized. I don't know whether it was because my mother wanted me to, the preacher expected me to, or all of my buddies were being baptized. All I know is, I was baptized.

I well remember one evening. I did a lot of my work at night in those days. I was in the cookware business, putting on demonstrations. I was coming in late one night from, I believe, Lancaster, South Carolina, (we lived in Columbia, a little town called Dent, just outside of Columbia). And I remember that evening turning left, right there at Dent, crossing the railroad tracks and turning right –I remember that.

The next thing I remembered I was being flagged down by the military police in Fort Jackson. I had driven straight for about six miles, I had turned left and the military police said I passed the outpost doing somewhere between 50 and 60 mph. I was so deep up into the Fort Jackson complex that they literally had to lead me out. I was absolutely lost.

Now there are a lot of people who will say, "Well, you know, you weren't really asleep." But when I got home that night the Redhead said to me, "Honey, I was praying unusually hard for you tonight." And those who would say, "You know you didn't really go to sleep." But I'm totally convinced that not only was I sound asleep, but I had the greatest chauffeur that any human being could ever have. God sent my angel, and he was driving that car. And he drove it beautifully.

Now you would have thought that with something like that, that at that point I would really make my commitment to Christ. But you see, I wanted to have some fun in life. I wanted to be successful. I wanted to make a lot of money. And obviously, Christians just don't do those things. I mean, let's face it: Christians go around with long faces and short pocketbooks. Now, everybody knows that. That was the image; that was the picture that I had of my own.

But on July the 4th, 1972, thanks to an elderly black lady, who spent the weekend in our home, we learned that number one, she was scripturally inaccurate. She claimed to be an angel, claimed to be a faith healer, claimed to be a prophet. We discovered she was none of those things. But there were two things we absolutely knew. Number one, she loved the Lord. And she loved me.

She walked into our home talking about Christ. She walked out of our home talking about Christ. And all during that weekend, all she talked about was Jesus Christ. My Savior came into my life in a very real way that weekend. I've always been grateful that she was not

46

prejudiced. Now almost immediately, my picture of being a Christian totally changed.

You know, I tell folks today, Christians ought to be kind of like the story of the Mama skunk and the Baby skunks going by the paper mill. How many of you have ever been close to a paper mill? Okay, you'll get the drift of this. One of the babies kind of sniffed the air and filled his nostrils with that pungent paper mill odor and said, "Mama, what on earth is that?" Well, the Mama skunk filled her nostrils with that pungent paper mill odor and said, "I don't know, but we sure got to get some of it!"

Now, you know, I believe–I believe that when people are Christians that somebody ought to have some way of knowing they are Christians. You know, you don't walk around looking like the cruise director for the Titanic—I mean, that is not my picture of what knowing Christ is all about. No, and I don't believe that either, that you're always grinning so wide you could eat a banana sideways. I don't believe that is in the picture either.

But there's an absolute joy that comes from knowing Christ that you will not experience anywhere else. When you know Christ, things are absolutely different. Christ manifested Himself in so many different ways almost immediately. It was almost as if He were saying, "Now I've let you fool around forty-five years of your life. Now I've got some things I want you to do, so I'm going to remove any doubt from your mind that your salvation is real."

Now I want to give you a little warning. Different people have different salvation experiences. Yours might be totally different from mine. You see, for mine, there was no "magic moment" on that weekend. I do not remember one minute being lost and the next minute being saved. But when I awakened on that Monday morning, I knew beyond any reasonable doubt that Christ was in my heart, that I'd made my commitment to Him, that I was a totally different human being.

Now the first thing I did on that morning was I went to my cabinet —now I was, at that time, a casual, social drinker. Now when I say "casual, social" I mean a maximum of three times a month and that was unusual. But in those days they used to give you the little small bottles on an airplane when you flew. If you didn't drink on the plane they'd give you two of them. I had a cabinet full of those things. I don't know if any of you remember seeing that airline movie where one of the flight attendants opened her closet and there were hundreds of those little bottles like mine. I had a case of champagne somebody had given to me. I had several other bottles and when I opened my cabinet door that morning I then headed for the sink with every one of those bottles and I dumped them down. No, now I don't believe drinking is going to send you to hell. I really don't. I don't believe smoking will. With smoking you smell like you've been there in advance. But anyhow . . . and you will get there quicker, you know, and so forth.

But you see, you don't go to hell because of what you do; you go to hell because of what you don't. And that simply is, believe. And I want to tell you how God used my son, who was seven years old, as a harassment committee of one to make absolutely certain that I walked a straight and narrow path. I well remember our anniversary that November after I-committed my life to Christ. We went out to a restaurant that was owned by the Redhead's hair-dresser. And he knew it was our anniversary. We got there and he gave us a bottle of wine.

Now I knew about my commitment that "never again." But I did not have the courage at that point to say to him, "No, we don't drink." And so the Redhead and I had a sample of that wine. I got home and that seven-year-old boy said to me, "Dad, did you drink any wine or anything?" And I said, "Yes, I did, son." And if I lived to be a thousand I'd never forget his exact words. He looked right at me and softly said, "Dad, I can't begin to tell you how disappointed I am in you."

I looked at my boy and I said, "Son, I'm going to make you a promise: If you'll forgive Dad this time, I promise you for the rest of my life I will never have to ask you to forgive me again." And I've kept that promise. Not in my strength, but in His.

After I was saved, I well remember, I was out in my swimming pool. I was looking up into the heavens. Really, I was praising God, and as I lay there I said, "God, I know you put this whole big, beautiful universe together and I know that one of these days you're going to take it down." And at that precise moment, a star fell. The God, I felt so close to, was speaking to me: "You're absolutely right boy, and don't you ever forget it." And I never have.

A few days later I had some time off. We decided to go down on a little trip. We drove down to Corpus Christi. And we spent a day there and then decided to go over to San Antonio. And as we headed to San Antonio my son said, "Dad, give me a Bible story." Well, you've got to understand that here's a boy whose dad had not been taking him to church, who has not been reading him the Bible and had not been praying with him.

You see, when we moved to Dallas in August of 1968 from Columbia, South Carolina, we didn't have any friends here. Nobody to say, "Well, let's go to church." Now in Columbia and other places we always had friends and always went to church, and we went to church because that was the thing to do. On several occasions, as I said earlier, I almost made a commitment. But now we come to Dallas, and no friends, and Sunday was the only day I had! I mean, you know, I want to do something for myself. And so we didn't go to church.

And now my boy says, "Dad, give me a Bible story." Well, fortunately, having been raised in the church I knew some Bible stories so I gave him one and he said, "Give me another one, Dad." I gave him another one. "Give me another one, Dad." I gave him another one. He said, "Give me another one, Dad." And about that time I was beginning to run out. And I said, "Well, boy, when we get to San Antonio I'll get the Book out and I'll give you more stories."

We got to San Antonio, checked in, went up to about the umpteenth floor and as the bellman set the bag down he said, "Okay, Dad, get the Book out and give me a story." I got the Book out and I did remember enough about the Bible. I went to the book of Exodus so I could get me a continuance story there. And I read, and finally, I said, "Boy, I'm hungry. We got to go get something to eat." And he said, "Okay, Dad. We'll take it up when we get back." Well we went to dinner and we came in, and the minute we walked in he said, "Okay, Dad. Get the Book out and give me some more stories."

I read until I absolutely got sleepy. I said, "Boy, I got to go to sleep." He said, "Okay, Dad. We'll take it up tomorrow." We got up the next day; we were going to drive back to Dallas and normally I drive. But as we headed for the car, he said, "Dad, I'll tell you what. Let's let Mom drive. You get the Book out; I want you to give me a story." God really was using him. You see, when you take that move toward God, you'll find He's already headed in your direction; He's been waiting for you all of your life.

(**Note 3**: www.zigziglarstory.com)

As a student of his masterful work, I am intrigued that his personal story may be the impetus for his compassion for people and his sheer desire to see them succeed in life. As a baby, Zig was pronounced dead on November 15, 1926, just nine days after his birth, by his family's physician. However, he was revived in his grandmother's arms and continued on to enjoy a long and fulfilled life that lasted for eighty-six years. Zig's many, many quotes have a way to inspire, encourage, and change your way of thinking to become a better you. Achieving success is one thing, but once you become successful you need to keep working at remaining successful both personally and professionally. Notice how some of Zig's most popular quotes focus on serving others and not himself:

Chart 4. – Famous Quotes by Zig

	Theme	Lesson Learned
"The foundation stones for a balanced success are honesty, character, integrity, faith, love, and loyalty."	Enjoy "balanced" success	Build a solid foundation that will stand the test of time through all of your relationships with others.
"You were born to win, but to be a winner, you must plan to win, prepare to win, and expect to win."	Work your plan and plan your work	As you win, help and serve others to achieve the same.
"Goals enable you to do more for yourself and others, too."	Do more...	Write (record) your goals, review them, then execute.
"It's not what you've got, it's what you use that makes a difference."	Your fulfillment is tied to your willingness to give of self to help others	Use your gifts, skills, abilities, and knowledge to help and service others.

Zig passed away in 2012, but these timely principles live on through the Zig Speaker Institute in Dallas, Texas. His legacy of service continues on.

Vince Lombardi: The Coach, the Leader, the Winner

*"People who **work together** will win, whether it be against complex football defenses or the problems of modern society."*

During his lifetime, Vincent Thomas Lombardi (Vince) was a National Football League (NFL) coach, notably for the Green Bay Packers, a team that he *led* to five championships. His effective and efficient leadership style was so infectious and impactful that in 1970, the league named its famous Super Bowl championship trophy after him: The Vince Lombardi Trophy. What made this great leader great?

In his early years, Lombardi screened Army game films for General Douglas McArthur. For a short time in the 1950s, he taught football in Japan. His preparation as a leader included a position as a high school assistant coach in Englewood, New Jersey, freshman as well as assistant football and basketball coach at Fordham University, assistant coach at the U.S. Military Academy at West Point, offensive coordinator for the New York Giants, before reaching his goal as head football coach for the Green Bay Packers (1959-1967) and Washington Redskins (1969-1970). During his tenure, he earned NFL Coach of the Year during his rookie season, won five NFL championships (this includes two Super Bowls – I & II), inducted as a charter member of the Fordham University Hall of Fame, named to the Pro Football Hall of Fame posthumously, inducted into the Green Bay Packers Hall of Fame and shortly after his death, the Rotary Club of Houston established the Lombardi Award, an annual honor that recognizes the nation's best collegiate lineman.

This consummate team builder and motivator inspired others as their coach to achieve their best because he recognized their value to the team. Because of this success, he became a national symbol of single-minded determination to win. Under Lombardi's leadership, the struggling Packers were transformed into hard-nosed winners. Over the course of his career with this team, he led the club to a 98-30-4 record, along with its five championships, including three straight titles, from 1965 to 1967. The team never suffered a losing season under the Hall of Fame coach. As a coach, general manager, and part-owner of the Washington Redskins, he led that team to its first winning season in fourteen years in 1969.

Lombardi's hundreds of documented quotes that demonstrate his commitment and faithfulness to *others* are recorded for all leaders, aspiring and seasoned, to read, apply, and execute. Some of the many include:

- **Success / Sacrifice**: *"Success is based upon a spiritual quality, a power to inspire others."*
- **Leadership**: *"Leadership is based on a spiritual quality – the power to inspire, the power to inspire others to follow."*
- **Excellence**:
  o *"They call it coaching but it is teaching. You do not just tell them...you show them the reasons."*
  o *"After all the cheers have died down and the stadium is empty, after the headlines have been written, and after you are back in the quiet of your room and the championship ring has been placed on the dresser and after all the pomp and fanfare have faded, the enduring thing that is left is the dedication to doing with our lives the very best we can to make the world a better place in which to live."*
- **Faith**: *"I believe in God."*
- **Passion:** *"To be successful, a man must exert an effective influence upon his brothers and upon his associates, and the degree in*

which he accomplishes this depends on the personality of the man. The incandescence of which he is capable of. The flame of fire that burns inside of him. The magnetism which draws the heart of other men to him."

- **Truth:** *"Faithfulness and truth are the most sacred excellences and endowments of the human mind."*

Simple Ideas, Deeply Understood

Lombardi reminds us that nearly every area of life can be boiled down to some core task or some essential component that must be mastered if you truly want to be good at it. They are:

<u>Fitness</u>: There are plenty of details you can focus on in the gym. Mobility work is great. Analyzing your technique can be important. Optimizing your programming is a good idea if you have the time and energy. However, these training details will never substitute for the one fundamental question that all athletes must answer: Are you stepping under the bar and getting your reps in?

<u>Love</u>: Displays of affection are wonderful. It's nice to buy your loved ones flowers or to spread joy with presents. Working hard for your family is admirable (and often very necessary). It's wonderful to upgrade to a larger house or to pay for your children's school or to otherwise advance to a higher standard of living. I'd like to do these things myself. But make no mistake, you can never buy your way around the most essential unit of love: showing up. To be present, this is love.

<u>Web Design</u>: Building a website is like painting on a canvas that never gets full. There is always space to add a new feature. There is never a moment when something couldn't be optimized or split-tested. But these details can distract us from the only essential thing that

websites do: communicate with someone. You don't need a fancy design or the latest software or faster web hosting to communicate with someone. The most basic unit of any website is the written word. You can do a lot with the right words.

Mastery in nearly any endeavor is the result of deeply understanding simple ideas. For most of us, the answer to becoming better leaders, better parents, better lovers, better friends, and better people is consistently practicing the fundamentals, not brilliantly understanding the details.

"This is a football."

Lombardi's championship pedigree was rooted in his training and passion to *serve*. Today, the Green Bay Packer organization is publicly-owned and they have won two Super Bowl championships under the leadership of two different quarterbacks since his death.

Zero Tolerance

On February 17, 2019, columnist Jena McGregor penned an article that reflects both the current state of affairs with our senior leaders and the swinging of the pendulum with regards to ethics and integrity—two of the highest characteristics. Its title, "CEOs in an Era of Zero Tolerance" centers on former REI Chief Executive Officer Jerry Stritzke who resigned his position because of a "perceived conflict of interest." This insightful piece reminds all leaders that questionable behavior must be reported to the board, especially in today's era of emphasis on executive integrity and zero tolerance for misbehavior.

Outdoor apparel and gear retailer REI acknowledged the resignation of their CEO on February 14, 2019, after a board investigation found that the relationship between him and "the leader of another organization in the outdoor industry" had not been disclosed. Although the inquiry found that no financial misconduct resulted from the relationship, "the facts led to a perceived conflict of interest," board chairman Steve Hooper wrote in a letter to employees "which he should have disclosed under the REO conflict of interest policy, which requires every REI executive to model the highest standard of conduct."

Further, Stritzke's resignation comes about seven months after Intel chief executive Brian Krzanich stepped down for violating a "non-fraternization" policy by having a consensual relationship with another employee. The CEOs of two other tech firms, Rambus and Texas Instruments, also departed last summer after unspecified conduct issues that either "fell short of the company's standards" or violated the code of conduct via personal behavior inconsistent with "our ethics and values." Last, in December, the CEO of electronics component supplier Kemet departed following an investigation of "a consensual personal relationship."

Some evidence appears to show an uptick in how much boards are cracking down on executive's conduct violations. A study by the PwC consulting arm Strategy&, in 2017, found that although the number of CEOs kicked out for ethical lapses is small (just 18 among the world's 2,500 largest public companies in 2016), they grew from 3.9 percent of all CEO hand-offs between 2007 and 2011 to 5.3 percent from 2012 to 2016, a 36 percent increase.

Following the departure of the Intel CEO, employment lawyer Valerie Hoffman with Seyfarth Shaw wrote that public company boards of directors now "have an extraordinary low tolerance for bad or non-compliant behavior by CEOs, even CEOs who are otherwise very successful. There has been a sea of change in this in the last 18 months."

(**Note 4:** *The Washington Post*, Section G (Metro) by Jena McGregor, February 17, 2019.)

Final Thoughts

Chapter one of this book sets the tone and premise of *servant leadership* with an emphasis on taking the focus off of ourselves and placing it on *serving* others. Jesus' teaching on this subject is clear, concise, and direct. If you desire to be great in your leadership acumen, abilities, and skills, then *serve* others and meet them at their place of need.

If anything is needed today, it is leaders who are willing to take a stand and do what is right whether or not it is politically correct. Leaders who are strong and courageous are very scarce, both in the world and in the church.

"It is absolutely clear that God has called you to a free life. Just make sure that you don't use this freedom as an excuse to do whatever you want to do and destroy your freedom. Rather, use your freedom to serve one another in love; that's how freedom grows. For everything we know about God's Word is summed up in a single sentence: Love others as you love yourself. That's an act of true freedom."

—Galatians 5:13-14 (The Message)

STUDY QUESTIONS & DISCUSSION

1. Identify two reasons you must treat others with *respect*.

_____

_____

_____

_____

_____

2. Do you give clear guidance when you *delegate* a task?

_____

_____

_____

_____

_____

3. How do you rate your *communication* skills?

_____

_____

_____

_____

_____

4. Do you believe that Biblical principles *enhance* your leadership skills?

_____

_____

_____

_____

_____

5. What can you do differently to *empower* others?

_____

_____

_____

_____

_____

CHAPTER TWO

How Do You Make Others Feel?

"Leaders must care. Leadership is about people. Period. Great leadership is about inspiring people, serving people, caring for people, and caring about people."

—Gary Kelly

Chairman and CEO, Southwest Airlines

"Not with eyeservice, as menpleasers; but as the servants of Christ, doing the will of God from the heart;"

—Ephesians 6:6 (King James Version)

I DO NOT WANT OTHERS TO feel what I felt while at work as a result of a senior-level leader's lack of sympathy during a tumultuous time of change.

It was during my brief tenure as a middle manager/director at a Fortune 1000 firm in New York City, that my colleagues and I suddenly learned about the previously unannounced merger and acquisition that would usher in unprecedented change into our functional and very efficient work environment. Our company had recently acquired a smaller business with a very similar mission and vision in the highly profitable fields of information technology and dissemination. The Senior Vice President who hired me and many of my peers just a few months prior to this merger and acquisition was kind, gentle, humble, supportive, and approachable. He had established key relationships at this company, knew its history, had developed a rapport with the senior leaders, understood the strategic priorities, and led my colleagues and me with passion, tact, professionalism, and diplomacy.

With the emergence of this merger, there were several business trips from St. Louis, Missouri, to New York City and back to discuss and negotiate the terms and conditions that would govern and solidify the deal. It was during these negotiations with my colleagues, including the legal teams from both companies, that our supervisor was fired and his replacement, also a Senior Vice President, would be appointed from the smaller company that was just acquired. He traveled with us as the new leader in charge of our unit Strategic Sourcing for the Americas. His leadership style was abrasive, rude, divisive, and sarcastic. Within his first two months as our new leader, he advised most but not all of us on his team that he had inherited, that his desire and hope was to replace us with others from his former company who he knew performed similar work. His *take-no-prisoners* approach to leadership alienated us, and he caused a rift in the workplace that ultimately led to a reduction in performance and productivity. There was a direct impact on our ability and desire to negotiate favorable contracts, achieve cost savings, generate new business, maintain rapport with existing clients, and embrace the change that was coming.

Feeling demoralized, shortly after the official merger I watched a few of my peers get escorted to the door by our security detail on a Friday afternoon during a time of layoffs. I wondered if these layoffs were a direct result of the new boss' desire to replace some. I will never know. The Human Resources Department's records are sealed. I do not recall all of the specific activities that took place during the transition, but I do remember, even until this day, how I felt as a result of how I and my peers were treated.

Equal Opportunity

Are we listening to those who we lead? Do we hear what others are saying taking into consideration how they feel resulting from our leadership or lack thereof?

The answer is *"no"* according to the U.S. Equal Employment Opportunity Commission (EEOC). Each year, the EEOC generates a report to summarize the collective views, statistics, and feedback from the 2.8 million employees of the federal government, excluding the military personnel. Workplace discrimination costs $64 billion per year to litigate and settle partly because leaders are not listening!

The EEOC is responsible for enforcing federal laws that make it illegal to discriminate against a job applicant or an employee because of the person's *race, color, religion, sex* (including pregnancy, gender identity, and sexual orientation), *national origin, age* (40 or older), *disability, or genetic information.* It is also illegal to discriminate against a person because the person *complained about discrimination, filed a charge of discrimination,* or *participated in an employment discrimination investigation or lawsuit.*

Most employers with at least fifteen employees are covered by EEOC laws (20 employees in age discrimination cases). Most labor unions and employment agencies are also covered. The laws apply to *all types of work situations*, including hiring, firing, promotions, harassment, training, wages, and benefits.

They have the authority to investigate charges of discrimination against employers who are covered by the law. Their role in an investigation is to fairly and accurately assess the allegations in the charge and then make a finding. If they find that discrimination has occurred, they will try to settle the charge. If unsuccessful, they have the authority to file a lawsuit to protect the rights of individuals and the interests of the public. They do not, however, file lawsuits in all cases where they find discrimination. EEOC also works to prevent discrimination before it occurs through outreach, education, and technical assistance programs. The EEOC provides leadership and guidance to federal agencies on all aspects of the federal government's equal employment opportunity program. EEOC assures federal agency and department compliance with EEOC regulations, provides technical assistance to federal agencies concerning EEO complaint adjudication, monitors and evaluates federal agencies' affirmative employment programs, develops and distributes federal sector educational materials, and conducts training for stakeholders, provides guidance and assistance to their Administrative Judges who conduct hearings on EEO complaints, and adjudicates appeals from administrative decisions made by federal agencies on EEO complaints.

EEOC Vision: *Justice and Equality in the Workplace*

EEOC Mission: *Stop and Remedy Unlawful Employment Discrimination*

A view into the EEOC's enforcement and litigation statistics (charges of employment discrimination and resolutions) show this startling data:

Chart 1. EEOC Enforcement and Litigation

	Fiscal Year 2013	Fiscal Year 2014	Fiscal Year 2015	Fiscal Year 2016
Total Charges	93,727	88,778	89,385	91,503
Race	33,088 (35.3%)	31,037 (35.0%)	31,027 (34.7%)	32,309 (35.3%)
Sex	27,687 (29.5%)	26,027 (29.3%)	26,396 (29.5%)	26,934 (29.34%)
National Origin	10,642 (11.4%)	9,579 (10.8%)	9,438 (10.6%)	9,840 (10.8%)
Religion	3,721 (4.0%)	3,549 (4.0%)	3,502 (3.9%)	3,825 (4.2%)
Color	3,146 (3.4%)	2,756 (3.1%)	2,833 (3.2%)	3,102 (3.48%)
Retaliation – Title VII only	31,478 (33.6%)	30,771 (34.7%)	31,893 (35.7%)	33,082 (36.2%)
Retaliation (All)	38,539 (41.1%)	37,955 (42.8%)	39,757 (44.5%)	42,018 (45.9%)
Age (40+)	21,396 (22.8%)	20,588 (23.2%)	20,144 (22.5%)	20,857 (22.8%)

This data _excludes_ disability, equal pay act, and the Genetic Information Nondiscrimination Act, Title II (2008).

(**Note 1**: www1.eeoc.gov//eeoc/statistics/enforcement/charges.cfm?renderforprint=1)

The Cost of Bad Leadership (United States)

There is further and disturbing evidence that the answer to the question, Are Leaders Listening? is a resounding '*no.*' The 12ᵗʰ Annual Workplace Class Action Litigation Report: 2006 Edition, summarizes a plethora of facts from hundreds of legal cases in their 863-page report by Seyfarth Shaw LLP, January 2016. This annual report analyzes the leading class action and collective action decisions of 2015 involving claims against employers brought in federal courts under Title VII of the Civil Rights Act of 1964, the Age Discrimination in Employment Act, the Fair Labor Standards Act, the Employee Retirement Income Security Act, and a host of other federal statutes applicable to workplace issues. The Report also analyzes class action and collective action rulings involving claims brought against employers in all 50 state court systems, including decisions pertaining to employment laws, wage and hour laws, and breach of employment contract actions. In total, there are 1,134 decisions analyzed in the report. As the evidence shows, poor and ineffective leadership costs. It costs in terms of lawsuits, legal representation, productivity, relationships, friendships, and our health (from worry, fear, discomfort, and uncertainty). Everyone pays! The 12ᵗʰ Annual Workplace Class Action Litigation Report: 2006 Edition, gives us clear and convincing data to support the extreme price tag that results from leadership styles that do not warrant the mistreatment of our fellow citizens and residents. Our natural reaction to less than fair and equitable is to fight back. Conversely, when treated with respect and dignity, followers will go out of their way to help their leader succeed. For example: in 2015 alone, as a nation, the U.S. spent close to $2.5 billion to settle lawsuits concerning mistreatment and unfair practices in the areas of employment, wage and hour, retirement income, statutory and governmental enforcement. Two and one-half billion dollars! Until this data improves, it supports the premise that leaders are not listening.

During my research on this subject, I highlight three specific trends from this detailed and comprehensive report:

Chart 2.

The total dollar amount of aggregate settlements overall increased from almost $2 billion in 2014 to almost $2.5 billion in 2015.

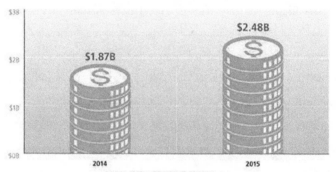

Aggregate Settlement Amounts

Chart 3.

The total dollar value of the Top 10 employment discrimination class action settlements decreased from 2010 to 2012, then spiked again from 2012 to 2015. In 2010, the value was highest at $346.4 million.

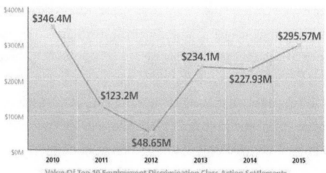

Value Of Top 10 Employment Discrimination Class Action Settlements

Chart 4.

The total dollar value of the top 10 government enforcement litigation settlements also shows a pattern of volatility from 2010 to 2015, reaching its highest value in 2012 (almost $300 million).

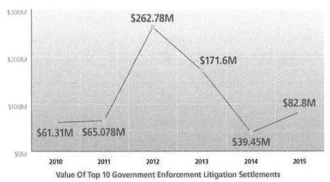

Value Of Top 10 Government Enforcement Litigation Settlements

The Cost of Bad Leadership (Worldwide)

The costs of liability systems can vary significantly from country to country with potential consequences for international competitiveness and productivity. Simply put, litigation costs affect the ability of companies to compete and prosper. But higher direct costs are just the tip of the iceberg: litigation also imposes indirect costs. These indirect costs stem from the uncertainty created by litigation, which may defer investment in high-cost jurisdictions. They also may affect companies' borrowing costs and hence their ability to invest, grow, and create jobs. Concerns surrounding litigation can also occupy management time which may distort or hinder effective business decision making.

Litigation costs affect the ability of companies to compete and prosper.

The report, *International Comparisons of Litigation Costs,* by NERA Economic Consulting provides a groundbreaking comparison of liability costs—a phrase used here to describe the costs of claims, whether resolved through litigation or other claims resolution processes—as a fraction of Gross Domestic Product (GDP) across Europe, the United States, Canada, and Japan. Businesses' general liability insurance costs provide a basis for comparing liability costs among countries with researchers controlling for non-litigation-related factors. Insurance costs are a meaningful basis for analysis because a large fraction of liability costs are covered by insurance, and coverage is sufficiently similar in Europe, the United States, Japan, and Canada. These countries also are generally similar in the scope of civil redress they provide for harm caused by third parties.

Key findings are as follows:

• The United States has the highest liability costs as a percentage of GDP compared to other countries surveyed (1.66%), with liability costs at 2.6 times the average level of the Eurozone economies.

• United States liability costs are four times higher than those of the least costly European countries in the study, namely, Belgium, the Netherlands, and Portugal.

• Although the United States has by far the most costly liability system, the analysis in the report shows that liability costs in the United Kingdom, Germany, and Denmark have risen between 13% and 25% per year since 2008.

• Japanese liability costs as a percent of GDP are lower than all of the other countries in the study, except for China. Changes in the legal environment in Japan that would encourage litigation could result in much higher liability costs.

• Features of the legal environment in each country are highly correlated with litigation costs, implying that changes to the liability system may have a substantial effect on costs. A common law (rather than civil law) tradition and a high number of lawyers per capita are strong indicators of higher litigation costs.

Chart 5. 2011 Liability Costs as a Fraction of GDP

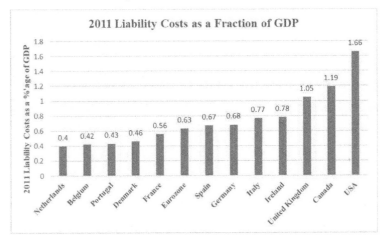

(**Note 2**: International Comparisons of Litigation Costs, U. S. Chamber Institute for Legal Reform)

Leaders: Pay Attention Please!

'Every week, I teach, coach, and train multiple diverse audiences on the principles and strategies that govern *servant leadership*. I am often requested to show evidence that leaders can cause irreparable harm to employees when they do not consider the short-term and long-term effects of misusing the authority and responsibility that comes with leadership. Three recent articles that I reference are:

a) Title: "Meet Workers Tossed Aside by the Strong Economy"

Columnist Andrew Van Dam writes: *The job market looks awesome. Unemployment is near its lowest since the 1960s. We're in the midst of the largest, longest streak of payroll growth in recorded history, and there are signs employers are finally raising wages. But the numbers obscure the experiences of millions of part-timers, temp, older workers and others who have done everything right but are still struggling to find good jobs. We heard from hundreds of them. Once we knew where to look, we found their stories right in front of us in the*

Labor Department's data.

  a. Ron Hartnett had a brain injury in 1973. Workplaces haven't always accommodated his disability, so he cobbles jobs together. He asks, "I did all that work for this amount?"

  b. Racquel Davis hopes to start a nonprofit to help women and minorities in STEM but now works part-time in a daycare. She asks, "You're going to pay me less to do the exact same work in Nashville?"

  c. Paul Corcoran waits for a ride-hail customer in Oceanside, California. Driving helps stretch his unemployment benefits. He states, "I'm not finding any interest in a 60-year-old guy with gray hair."

Van Dam shares that for older workers, their numbers are growing rapidly, but their earnings aren't. Part-time workers are here to stay and earn less. Temp workers are more numerous than ever. For the unemployed, it still takes longer to find work. Finally, for construction workers, they are having trouble finding new jobs.

(**Note 3**: *The Washington Post*, Metro Section, July 29, 2018, by Andrew Van Dam)

  b) Title: "47% Rise in Students Facing Unwanted Sexual Contact at Military Academies," by Paul Sonne and Dan Lamothe

In the spirit of this title, the alarming details that impact loyal and dedicated women of the armed forces should startle leaders that represent a diversity of industries (church, corporations, non-profits, and government).

It reads in part: *The estimated number of men and women experiencing unwanted sexual contact in the U.S. military's service academies jumped 47 percent since the figures were last gathered two years ago, raising concerns about the Pentagon's efforts to reduce sexual violence among the future leaders of the U.S. armed forces. According to the survey, which the Defense Department released Thursday, an estimated 747 cadets and midshipmen at the military's three service academies – U.S. Military Academy at West Point; the U.S.*

Naval Academy in Annapolis, Maryland; and the U.S. Air Force Academy in Colorado Springs, Colorado - experienced unwanted sexual contact during the 2017-2018 academic year, up from 507 cadets and midshipmen two years ago. The analyses uses the term "unwanted sexual contact" to encompass a wide range of sex-related offenses they said were prohibited by the Uniform Code of Military Justice. Mr. Nate Galbreath, Pentagon's Sexual Assault Prevention Office, stated, "This is really disheartening for us because the strategies that we put in place aren't having the effect that we intended."

The article concludes with the following statement from the Defense Department: *The survey was conducted before the military service academies implemented mandated plans in the summer of 2018 to address sexual harassment and sexual assault. As a result, the Pentagon cautioned that the results didn't "reflect the large investment of attention, time and resources dedicated to these problems."*

Really?

(**Note 4:** *The Washington Post*, A Section, February 1, 2019)

c) Title: "The Federal Workforce's Shrinking Morale" (editorial)

As a career federal government employee at the mid-level and senior-level ranks, this insightful and thought-provoking editorial caught my immediate attention on a Monday morning. The subtitle captured the core of the content and overarching message that should resonate with all leaders. The subtitle, *A survey of job satisfaction at government agencies shows the adverse effect of Mr. Trump's hostile rhetoric,* highlights the feelings of a large group of workers as a direct result of the words from their leader, the Commander in Chief.

The editorial reads in part: *President Trump said last week he would be "proud" to shut down the federal government – and when the boss has an attitude like that, it is no surprise that federal employees*

71

take somewhat less pride in laboring for their employer. The nonpartisan Partnership for Public Service released its annual survey charting employee morale across government agencies last Wednesday, and after three years of post-recession progress, the numbers have dipped. Less than 40 percent of agency ratings increased, compared to more than 70 percent in the past three years. The public sector is constantly competing against a private sector that often can offer higher salaries, and numbers such as this year's suggest the government will continue to lose. There's no doubt that the administration's anti-"deep state" rhetoric repels the national resource of smart, civic-minded Americans deciding where to take their skills. But there are steps the government can take to guard against workforce depletion, notwithstanding a hostile president. That starts with bringing in younger workers; only 6 percent of federal employees are under age 30. Fresh technical talent is especially lacking: Nearly five times more IT employees are 60 or older than under the age of 30.

This is a big problem. Of course, morale still matters.

(**Note 5:** *The Washington Post,* A Section, December 17, 2018)

Gary Kelly – Customers and Employees Deserve the Best Treatment

Southwest Airlines was established in 1967 and is the premier low-cost air carrier in the United States. It has a fleet of 579 airplanes and flies between 89 destinations as of 2013. It is credited as being the highest used airline by U.S. citizens for domestic flights. It operates nearly 3,400 flights each day. In 2012, it had a yearly revenue of $17 billion and currently has more than 45,000 employees. It is one of the most-loved airlines in the U.S. because of its low cost, safety, and customer care oriented service.

On March 16, 1967, Air Southwest Co. was incorporated by entrepreneur Rollin King and lawyer Herb Kelleher. They came across the idea of starting a low-cost airline between San Antonio, Dallas, and Houston in Texas. Some of the heavyweights in the industry tried to ground them by filing legal suits against them. But after three years of a heated battle, the U.S. Supreme Court allowed Air Southwest to continue its services without any penalty. In March 1971, Air Southwest Co. officially became Southwest Airlines Co. It operated three Boeing 737-200's across its three destinations with over 60 flights per week. Southwest was always put into trouble by other big airlines who did not want Southwest's industry-changing strategy to be implemented. But with Herb Kelleher at Southwest Airways, legal troubles could not trouble them for long. In 1973, Southwest was profitable for the first time and has been so ever since until 2013. Southwest's business strategy is the reason for its tremendous growth. When they were forced to fly an empty plane back to Dallas for weekend servicing, they took advantage of that opening and priced tickets at $10. In the space of weeks, this flight was flying without a spare seat.

> "One of the most rewarding aspects of Leadership is being part of a Team, and I am so grateful to be a part of the Southwest Team serving you today."
>
> Gary Kelly

Southwest's rate cuts did not need any advertisements but spread quickly through word of mouth. Soon they increased the regular rates to $26 from $20 and the $10 ticket to $13. Their competitors were forced to decrease their prices as well. But one airline decreased its regular fare to $13 to attract customers off Southwest. At every step, Southwest faced stiff opposition but came out trumping their opponents. By 1982, it was able to expand itself to more than 22 new cities including Oklahoma, San Diego, Las Vegas, Phoenix, and New Orleans. By 1989, it had crossed $1 billion in revenues. By the year 1992, Southwest was carrying more than 30 million customers a year and had become the seventh-largest airline in the U.S. By now it had crossed the $2 billion revenue mark and had 15,000 full-time staff working for them. In 1995, Southwest was one of the first airlines to use a website as a means for showing flight schedules, route map, and other useful information. By 2006, nearly 65% of the flight bookings for Southwest Airways were completed on-line (www.southwest.com). Southwest's success is the result of bringing in the latest innovations to make the airline industry *customer-centric*. It has been a super successful company becoming one of the most loved airlines in the U.S.

(**Note 6**: https://successstory.com/companies/southwest-airlines-co)

Gary's Greeting - Five Characteristics of Effective Leaders by Gary Kelly

For as long as I can remember, I have studied and admired Leaders. In grade school, I began reading biographies of the presidents of the United States, and ever since, I have studied Leaders from all walks of life – from politics to the corporate world. I've also been blessed to have had wonderful Leaders and mentors during my career, especially our Founder and Chairman Emeritus, Herb Kelleher, and our President Emeritus, Colleen Barrett. Through these lifelong studies, I've seized on five characteristics critical to being a successful Leader:

1. **Leaders must care.** *Leadership is about people. Period. Great Leadership is about inspiring people, serving people, caring for people, and caring about people. You have to show you care through daily actions.*

2. **Leaders must communicate.** *Not communicating well is one of the great mistakes a Leader can make. When Leaders don't communicate well, Employees don't feel valued. For that reason, I can't*

think of anything more important in Leadership than communication. Good communication involves listening and genuinely respecting others' opinions.

3. **Leaders must have character.** *To be a great Leader of Team Member, you must have character: honesty, integrity, respect for others, and selflessness. There's an old saying that adversity doesn't create character, it reveals it.*

4. **Leaders must be competent.** *Effective Leaders know their stuff. You must be competent. Under-promise and over-prepare. I've found that the technical aspects of a profession are the easier parts, and the human relationship side is the most challenging. Still, you must be competent and proficient to get anything done.*

5. **Leaders must have courage.** *Finally, Leaders must have courage. It's easier to be a follower and let someone else own a problem or make a decision. It's much harder to stand up, speak up, and be accountable.*

A Southwest Story

Is it true that Southwest Airlines interrupted a takeoff to re-ticket a passenger because her son had suffered a serious head injury and was in a hospital in another part of the country? This story most likely came out because of all the problems the airline industry has had after highly publicized reports of United Airlines' forcibly removing a passenger from a flight and Delta Air Line's booting a family off an overcrowded flight and threatening them with jail time.

Various online sources began reporting the "recent" heartwarming story about Southwest Airlines: *"United Airlines has probably made you sick of reading about airlines by now, but we promise this story is a good one. Recently, Peggy Uhle was boarding a flight from Chicago to*

Columbus, Ohio. She decided to turn off her cell phone as the plane rolled away from the gate (talk about a good passenger). The plane went through its safety protocol and was ready for take-off, but it wasn't long until the plane decided to turn back around on the tarmac at Midway Airport and taxi back toward the gate. Peggy and other passengers were very confused as to what was going on. Once the plane was anchored at the gate again, a flight attendant approached Peggy and asked her to get off. When she got back inside the terminal, a gate agent told her to call her husband. He had been forced to contact Southwest Airlines because Peggy's phone was turned off. ...It turned out that Peggy's 24-year-old son had suffered a serious head injury and was in a coma in Denver, Colo. But wait, there's more. As Peggy was trying to take in the shocking news, a staffer explained that the airline had re-ticketed her on the next direct flight to Denver and arranged all of the other details for her. All for free."

Uhle said the airline rerouted her luggage, allowed her to board first, and packed a lunch for when she got off the plane in Denver. Her luggage was delivered to where she was staying, and Southwest called her to ask how her son was doing. Her son did recover from his injuries making for a happy ending to a story.

This tale wasn't really "recent," Snopes.com found. It occurred and was originally reported nearly two years earlier on May 27, 2015, by Chicago station WGN. *"We're certainly proud of, but not surprised by, any of the hard work that went into doing the right thing for Ms. Uhle and her family,"* said Southwest spokesperson Thais Hanson in a statement to WGN.

The airline, which has a policy of no change fees, never asked to be repaid for the rebooking.

"This example is a direct reflection of the Southwest Airlines

culture," Hanson said. "*Employees are empowered at Southwest to go above and beyond the call of duty and follow their hearts to make decisions that positively impact our customers.*"

(**Note 7**: http://jacksonville.com/reason/2017-05-13/fact-check-story-true-about-southwest-s-benevolence)

Chick-Fil-A – A Case Study in Employee Relations

In 2006, for the very first time, Chick-fil-A sales surpassed \$2.0 billion securing the family-owned company as a billion-dollar brand.

Chick-fil-A, Inc., Founder S. Truett Cathy started the business in 1946 when he and his brother Ben opened an Atlanta diner known as The Dwarf Grill (later renamed The Dwarf House®). Through the years that restaurant prospered and led Cathy to further the success of his business. In 1967, Cathy founded and opened the first Chick-fil-A restaurant in Atlanta's Greenbriar Shopping Center. Today, Chick-fil-A has the highest same-store sales and is the largest quick-service chicken restaurant chain in the U.S. based on annual system-wide sales.

Cathy is the author of six books and is a committed philanthropist dedicated to making a difference in the lives of youth. He is the recipient of countless awards over the years both for his business acumen and for his charity. With his wife Jeannette McNeil Cathy of sixty-five years, he led a life that was centered on biblical principles and family.

Humble Beginnings. At the age of eight, young Truett Cathy experienced the feel-good power of *customer service*. He was selling Coca-Colas door-to-door, buying a six-pack of Cokes for a quarter and selling them for a nickel each. It was the summer of 1929 before air conditioning and even refrigerators entered many homes, and every afternoon the lady who lived across the street from the Cathy's sat on her front porch drinking a Coke. But she wasn't buying them from

Cathy. Somehow, he had to add value to his product to convince her to buy his Cokes. One day his neighbor told him that he could sell more Cokes if he would ice them down. Taking her advice, he set up shop in the front yard and chipped some ice from his mother's icebox to chill his Cokes. Not only did his neighbor buy from him, but so did other people coming home on hot afternoons. They were happy to pay a nickel for cool refreshment, and the young Cathy experienced the joy of making his customers' day.

Finding Friendships through Service. A few years later when he was a teenager delivering newspapers, Cathy treated each customer as though he or she was the most important person in the world. *"I delivered each paper as if I were delivering it to the front door of the governor's mansion,"* he said. He made sure they didn't have to dig through the bushes for their paper, and on rainy days he found a dry spot at every door. Though he didn't have as much face-to-face contact with his newspaper customers, they expressed their appreciation when collection day came. Over the years, those and other experiences reinforced Cathy's deep *love for customers*. When he and his brother Ben opened a 24-hour restaurant in 1946, they worked alternating 12-hour shifts. *"We built our business and made friends at the same time, always seeking to meet their needs wherever we could,"* Cathy would recall years later. If they learned that a customer was in the hospital, they sent food to the family. They did the same for customers' families when someone would pass away.

When Cathy began opening Chick-fil-A restaurants, he selected local franchise owners who shared his *love for people*. He saw that love expressed in the obvious ways and the not-so-obvious. Remembering the days when he treated every newspaper customer like the governor, *he suggested his restaurant owners and team members treat every person who walked through their doors like the president.* If the president walked into the restaurant, he wrote in his book *Eat Mor Chikin: Inspire More People, "Your voice and facial expressions would change. You'd be eager to serve the president well, make sure he had a clean table, then go up and see if everything was all right, or if he needed anything. If we're willing to do that for the president, why not treat every customer that well?"*

Making it a Pleasure to Serve. One of Cathy's simplest expressions of love has become a memorable part of the Chick-fil-A experience: *"My pleasure."* Cathy was visiting a high-end hotel, and when he thanked an employee the man helping him replied genuinely, *"My pleasure."* Cathy felt his sincerity, and the memory of the man's smile and those two little words stayed with him for several days. He decided to ask his restaurant owners, team members, and even his corporate staff to respond with *"My pleasure"* whenever someone said thank you. *"You expect that from a five-star hotel,"* Cathy said. *"But to have teenagers in a fast-food atmosphere saying it's their pleasure to serve—that's a real head-turner."* *"My pleasure"* became an expression of *love for customers.* Almost immediately Cathy began receiving letters from customers telling him about their experiences after hearing restaurant team members say those magic words. It was genuine, and customers knew it.

Through the years Cathy found many other ways to have fun with customers. When the Chick-fil-A cows were introduced in 1995, he quickly learned that the cows made people laugh. So wherever he went, he always brought at least one bag of small plush cows in the trunk of his car. He would walk into a Chick-fil-A restaurant or even an airport carrying a bag of cows and passing them out—especially to children. But never before asking, *"What do the cows say?"* When he heard the right answer (Eat more chicken, obviously), then he shared another cow and another smile. While opened only six days per week, Chick-fil-A still outpaces Kentucky Fried Chicken in sales!

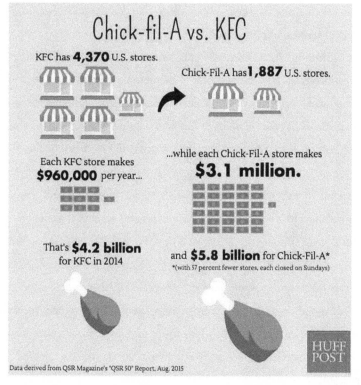

Chick-fil-A vs. KFC

KFC has **4,370** U.S. stores.

Chick-Fil-A has **1,887** U.S. stores.

Each KFC store makes **$960,000** per year...

...while each Chick-Fil-A store makes **$3.1 million.**

That's **$4.2 billion** for KFC in 2014

and **$5.8 billion** for Chick-Fil-A*
*(with 57 percent fewer stores, each closed on Sundays)

HUFF POST

Data derived from QSR Magazine's "QSR 50" Report, Aug. 2015

Employees. Creating the Chick-fil-A® Chicken Sandwich led to one of Chick-fil-A Founder Truett Cathy's greatest unexpected opportunities—the chance to have a positive influence on hundreds of thousands of employees who would work in Chick-fil-A restaurants over the years. Especially for teenagers. Cathy always had a heart for young people. For fifty years he taught thirteen-year-old boys in his church and became a mentor to dozens of them. And though he did not have direct contact with all of those restaurant team members in his restaurants, his influence in selecting and coaching his local restaurant owners created an atmosphere where people truly enjoyed working while learning strong work habits and positive attitudes. *"They will be adults in the business world,"* Cathy wrote in his book *Eat Mor Chikin: Inspire More People. "Even when they're not with Chick-fil-A, we want them to have fond memories of having worked for us,"* says Cathy.

A Helping Hand. And he wanted them to find success. Not having the opportunity to attend college himself, Cathy established a college scholarship program in 1973 for restaurant team members. Cathy wanted to encourage restaurant employees to further their education. Over time, the scholarship program evolved to place greater emphasis on an employee's community service and leadership abilities. His goal: encourage the qualities that would help them not only be successful in school but also in life. After all, Chick-fil-A restaurants, Cathy believed, should be places *where leaders develop future leaders.* In fact, his first gauge of his restaurant owners' success was not profits or sales, but the number of future Chick-fil-A restaurant owners that started their careers in that restaurant. In his own first restaurant, the Dwarf House, Cathy earned a reputation for having a heart for his employees. Eddie White, a teenager working in the Dwarf House in the 1950s, hoped to attend college, but he needed financial help. The waitresses put an empty mayonnaise jar labeled "Eddie's College Fund" on the counter for customers who felt like family to fill up. In the fall of 1955 when it was time to start college, the jar had not collected enough, so Truett wrote a check for the difference—his first scholarship. White completed college and went on to a career as a classroom educator, and ultimately an assistant superintendent of a school system near Atlanta.

Creating a Day of Rest. Some of Cathy's most significant business decisions were made with employees in mind. For example, his decision to close on Sundays, a practice started to give restaurant employees (and himself) a day to rest. Cathy started the practice when he had only one restaurant, and as he opened new Chick-fil-A restaurants, the malls where his restaurants were located pressured Cathy to open on Sundays. He refused. Chick-fil-A restaurant owners and team members knew they could count on at least one day each weekend they could devote to resting, friends, family, and personal pursuits. *"This is one of the most important principles we live by,"* Cathy often said. *"Family must come first."* Cathy also believed that *people want to work for a person, not a company. "The more we can foster the feeling that we are a group of people working together depending on each other,"* he said, *"the more likely we are to be loyal to each other."*

> Some of Cathy's most significant business decisions were made with employees in mind.

Creating a Legacy of Kindness. In the early days of the Dwarf House, Truett hired employees who worked with him for decades. When she retired after forty-five years at the Dwarf House, Zelma Calhoun told an Atlanta newspaper, *"I've never heard Mr. Cathy raise his voice. I don't remember him arguing with anybody. I've never heard him tell somebody to do something. He would ask. He'd say, 'Zelma, would you make me such-and-such a pie? Is that a problem?' Well, you had to do it, because he asked so nice."* Likewise, many of his restaurant owners and corporate staff worked their entire careers with Chick-fil-A, or rather, with Cathy. The loyalty he fostered had as much personal benefit as it did practical. He believed that when people are happy in their work, they respond by taking great care of customers. Of all the awards Truett received, one he was particularly proud of was the

National Caring Award given by the Caring Institute. *"That's really the key,"* Cathy said. *"Caring."*

Final Thoughts

In Chapter 2, we examined the question that every leader should consider: *"How do you make others feel?"* It's an important and relevant question that aids in understanding and improving listening skills.

The data published by the EEOC is undeniably disturbing. People in the workplace take formal action against their leaders because of how they *feel*. The high cost of litigation that results from these official actions has risen substantially over the past nine years. According to a statement titled "Litigation Cost Survey for Major Companies," by Lawyers for Civil Justice, Civil Justice Reform Group, U.S. Chamber Institute for Legal Reform, May 10-11, 2010, the average outside litigation cost per respondent was nearly $115 million in 2008, up from $66 million in 2000. This represents an average increase of 9 percent each year.

I signal a warning to all leaders to pay attention to their individual and collective leadership styles. If your approach is not generating efficiencies, then make a change. Follow the Southwest Airlines and Chick-Fil-A models of customer service and treatment of employees that have been proven to work effectively and are based upon trust, honesty, value, and courtesy.

Listening builds trust which is the foundation of all lasting and meaningful relationships.

STUDY QUESTIONS & DISCUSSION

1. Do you currently *value* and *appreciate* those who you are entrusted to lead?

_____

_____

_____

_____

_____

2. Do you take sufficient time to *listen* to others?

_____

_____

_____

_____

_____

3. Do your followers *trust* you? How do you know?

_____

_____

_____

_____

4. Name two strategies that you will implement to build trust in your organization.

_____

_____

_____

_____

_____

5. How do you *measure* the quality of your relationships?

_____

_____

_____

_____

_____

CHAPTER THREE

Celebrate Their Potential

"A successful person finds the right place for himself. But a successful leader finds the right place for others."

"To add value to others, one must first value others."

—John C. Maxwell
The world's #1 Leadership Expert

"Trust in the Lord with all your heart and lean not on your own understanding; in all your ways submit to him, and he will make your paths straight."

—Proverbs 3:5-6 (New International Version)

MY JOURNEY IN LEADING OTHERS

On October 31, 2017, I officially retired after thirty-four years of total service with the federal government. This includes a brief time of three years with a Fortune 1000 firm as a mid-level manager.

My full-time journey began in 1984 with desires and aspirations to serve as a senior executive at some point in time during my career. To achieve this lofty goal, I needed to learn how to lead and understand the tenets of successful leadership. As one of my many mentors taught me early in my career, *"Earn the trust of your people and they will do the work."*

Relationship building at the Defense Personnel Support Center in south Philadelphia, Pennsylvania, began immediately with my class of twenty-five interns. The year was 1984 and I was a grade 5 entry-level civilian employee. I learned the first names of my new classmates within two weeks, befriended them on a personal basis, ate lunch with them, and occasionally visited a local restaurant after class or work, paving the way to get to know them beyond the workplace. I got to know them as 'people,' not just classmates or colleagues. This practice became routine with my leadership style as I moved on following graduation from the Defense Logistics Agency acquisition intern program to Manassas, Virginia, in 1987. In this new environment, collocated with government corporate personnel at IBM Corporation, I was in the midst of a mixed group of military, corporate, and government personnel. Within a relatively short period of time, it became clear that the mannerisms and behaviors that I exhibited in Philadelphia could work in Manassas as well. After all, they are people with the same basic needs and goals. I progressed from grade 5 to grade 12 during this tenure in my career (1984 – 1989), in part, as a demonstration of my acumen *and* leadership approach/style.

Following this journey during the early years in my government career, I advanced into the mid-level managerial ranks that really opened my eyes. It was during this phase that I transitioned into my first leadership position following graduation from the government's

Executive Potential Program in New York City. The workplace was adversarial, management was pitted against the powerful labor unions, and I was instantly treated as the enemy by the union stewards because I was a manager. The environment there assumed that all managers, seasoned and new, were the bad guys based upon the history of the previous relationships. It took three years to convince both my staff and the union stewards that I meant no harm to any of the employees there. Relationship building and consistency of purpose were the hallmarks that separated me from the other managers in the workplace. My staff also took notice of my persistent intentions to mentor the next leader since they were aware of my departure within thirty-six months from the time that I first arrived. When I left this particular job in 1999, I ensured that the deputy of the office was equipped to lead the team.

At the turn of the millennium, local corporations were recruiting me with their large salaries and annual bonuses. I admit that these salaries were very attractive, and I gave in to their aggressive recruitment efforts. From 1999 to 2003, while entrusted with key positions and responsibilities including Acting Senior Director for the Americas at a Fortune 1000 firm, I was not successful with embracing people on a personal level (my usual leadership style) because the company did not embrace it. The company's culture demanded "results" by any means necessary, mandated precision intelligence on the topic of the day, and earning revenues for the company at all costs. Any employee who failed to produce by their standards was laid off or fired! I watched some of my peers escorted out of the front door and listened as they were told that their personal belongings would be mailed to them within a few days.

As I matriculated back into the federal government ranks in 2003 as a grade 15, I refocused my efforts and approaches to leadership principles and strategies that worked during my entry-level and mid-level years. Again, I witnessed phenomenal results. With each position at the senior-level that I held, I hired an applicant who our organization needed to be successful then I trained and mentored them all to become the leader when I departed for my next assignment. In my last position as Chief of Staff, Department of Defense, Expeditionary Operations Support Group, I hired an information technology expert as my deputy so that our organization could begin a records management program as required by law. As we worked together and cooperatively for two years, I trained her to become the next Chief of Staff as I was planning to retire. The leaders of the organization accepted my recommendation and she did a magnificent job in that role.

The key take away from my thirty-four-year career in the federal government is to always treat others in the same manner in which you want to be treated. It works. I know.

The Impact of Transformational Change at General Electric

John Francis "Jack" Welch, Jr. is a retired business executive, author, and chemical engineer. He was Chairman and Chief Executive Officer (CEO) of General Electric (GE) between 1981 and 2001. During his tenure at GE, the company's value rose 4,000%. Welch's transformative leadership style, in large part, contributed to the company's track record of tapping into its workforce, leadership team, and customer base potential. Let's explore how he accomplished such a feat as CEO of this Fortune 100 firm for twenty years. Leadership style axiom numbers 1, 2, 7 and 9 are most noteworthy:

Eleven Leadership Style Axioms

During his tenure at GE, he was both praised and criticized for his management style. Unwavering from what his critics were saying about how he led the company, Welch was able to co-author a book with his third wife, Suzy Welch, former *Harvard Business Review* editor and founded an online executed MBA program at Chancellor University, the Jack Welch Management Institute (JWMI). He was tagged as an icon and a transformative leader in the business world who made a change in American corporate management equipped with his innovative and grounded leadership styles. Other businesses have adopted his management strategies, a gauge that he was able to yield results. Welch's 11 leadership style axioms are:

1. One of his legacies is an organizational behavior he referred to as "boundaryless."

For Welch, there should never be a reason for great ideas not to be *shared with every member of the organization,* whether it is the manager or a rank and file employee. Consequently, he went beyond traditional functions and pointed out that ideas should be searched, whether from other businesses or the different departments in the organization, and conveyed to the team. He believed more in *leading* than managing.

2. He believed that performing employees and managers should be rewarded and inefficient ones should be terminated.

This management style was first called "vitality curve" and acquired the term "rank and yank" after some time. During his leadership at GE, *he rewarded managers who belonged to the top 20% with higher compensation and bonuses* while he let go those who were in the bottom 10%. This resulted in a big reduction in the number of employees in 1985.

3. He encouraged informality in the office.

Welch believed in simplicity when it comes to management. He was not a fan of complexity and started a signature campaign to simplify things in the organization. Complicated letters and memos were eliminated under his management. Just like Google and Facebook, he encouraged more comfortable clothes devoid of ties at the office. He also allowed brainstorming among executives and colleagues.

4. With his determination to take the company to the top, he was seen as lacking empathy on the working class.

Whenever they acquired other businesses or underwent mergers with other organizations, he did not have any qualms to terminate employees who he thinks were not needed. He did not exhibit hesitation to reduce the number of employees because for the corporate genius, retaining a few but good people in an organization is important.

5. He pushed for the elimination of bureaucracy at the office.

The former GE CEO was not a fan of following strict rules or processes to get work done. For him, it is important to work on necessary things. Unlike a bureaucratic organization which has levels when it comes to addressing problems with issues being escalated to the person or department responsible, a less formal practice allows members of the organization to communicate with each other.

6. Jack Welch, as the man on top of GE, was a doer and a realist.

He encouraged his team to act on what is at hand and see the facts. For him, there is no room for assumptions but for options. He got rid of bureaucracy and instead came up with strategies to accomplish work faster. Critics claim that this management style led some of his employees to cut corners when it comes to their jobs.

7. He welcomed change.

Although not all were supportive of this outlook, Welch made drastic changes within the organization which he believes were instrumental to the success of the company under his management. He was not scared to sell businesses which he thought were not doing great. Also, he reduced basic research.

8. He was not scared to buy and sell companies.

While with GE, he was able to acquire RCA but did not hesitate to sell its properties. He was also not afraid to take the company to the next level by giving up manufacturing and concentrating on financial services through the acquisition of other businesses.

9. He was far from being a micro-manager because he believed that members of the team should be given autonomy when it comes to decision-making.

Managers, according to him, should be leaders and the visionaries of organizations. He also knew the importance of providing employees with tools and skills to be better at their jobs. *Delegation is one of the management styles he supported and argued that managers should empower their subordinates instead of overpowering them and doing all the tasks.*

10. He was a believer of prioritizing values over figures.

Jack Welch, of course, had always been firm in saying that people should work to make the business number one or at least, number two. However, he also emphasized the significance of keeping customers happy being open to new ideas and eliminating bureaucracy. He placed more emphasis on these things than on how much money the company was making. Ironically, this leadership style contributed to making GE a manufacturing giant.

11. Jack Welch pushed his employees to be active members of the team and keep up with competitors.

He encouraged his office workers to be on their toes at all times and not be slowed down by decision-making. What he wanted was for employees to be quick in making decisions but also be prudent. He reiterated that it is good to have short-term plans, but it is best to plan long-term while one is busy with things at hand.

Jack Welch believed in controlling one's destiny. His leadership strategies might be too harsh and cold to critics but his style worked. Considered to be an incremental leader, Welch is not one who finds joy in being dormant. He led by example and lived by his principles, making him a very influential figure in corporate America.

(**Note 1**: Joseph Chris, August 20, 2015)

How Jack Welch Used Transformational Leadership Theory to Turn Around GE

In an article discussing leadership theories and styles that employees will respond to, CEO and Managing Partner Beth Williams briefly discusses motivational or transformational leadership theory. The defining characteristics of this type of leadership are that they are executed with:

- Vision and passion
- Enthusiasm and energy
- Care for those for whom the leader has responsibility

Putting Transformational Leadership Theory Into Action

Executing transformational leadership theory requires the leader to be a constant advocate of the future vision. He or she will prove to be a sponsor who can jump-start change by being visible, being committed to strategy and plans, yet able to empathize with employees, customers, and other stakeholders. The executive who best executes transformational leadership theory thrives on challenge but understands that people may be resistant to change and so develops the necessary negotiating skills to smooth the path of change management.

Jack Welch: The Master of Transformational Leadership Theory

Of all business leaders who have executed organizational change, perhaps Jack Welch stands head and shoulders above his peers. When asked to summarize his approach, he showed that he completely understood that great leadership begins with the development of high emotional intelligence. Welch sees the process of leading an organization in four simple steps:

- Start by working on yourself.
- Encourage your people to take the initiative.
- Use the brains of every worker.
- Create an atmosphere where workers feel free to speak out.

Leading GE to Glory

When Welch became CEO of General Electric, what he found was a multi-layered hierarchical animal in which decisions were never made. Nine layers of management meant that communication was fractured. The company's mission and vision were non-existent, and people simply turned-up and then went home again. Inevitably, the spectra of bankruptcy hung over the company like the grim reaper waiting to pounce. Welch immediately rolled up his sleeves and went out into the field. He made sure that everyone in the company called him Jack. During his redesign of corporate structure, not only did he remove multiple management layers but he also insisted that executives acted with the same informality as Welch did. He sent them into factories, regional offices, and work floors with instructions to observe and listen. Instead of team meetings being led by middle managers and a time for employees to receive orders, they became sounding boards for the discussion of problems and the debate of solutions. *Collaboration became a keyword for success.* Welch spoke directly to his people and likened GE to a local grocery store. He put customer satisfaction at the heart of the GE mission saying, *"If the customer isn't satisfied, if the stuff is getting stale, if the shelf isn't right, or if the offerings aren't right, it's the same thing."*

Transforming Leadership.

Jack Welch would make regular appearances at the GE management training center, speaking to dozens of GE managers simultaneously. He'd remove his jacket and roll up his sleeves, symbolically saying *"we're in this together, and we should all be prepared to get our hands dirty."* Welch would speak and listen. He encouraged managers to talk freely, sharing their fears, concerns, and knowledge. The managers present saw Welch as a human being and became willing participants on his voyage of discovery. By listening to them he identified GE's weaknesses and opportunities and was able to negotiate a breakdown of management's resistance to change. During his time as GE's CEO, Welch interacted with more than 15,000 GE executives at the company's training center. Every time he did so, he showed the same passion and enthusiasm for the GE mission and his vision of the future. He encouraged all of GE's executives to cascade the message and methods down through the organization. He regularly followed up with impromptu visits, emails, and phone calls. He broke the cumbersome hierarchy, removed red-tape, and destroyed the 'them-and-us' attitude that had existed previously. He later said, *"The story about GE that hasn't been told is the value of an informal place. I think it's a big*

> *"Before you are a leader, success is all about growing yourself. When you become a leader, success is all about growing others."*
> Jack Welch

thought. I don't think people have ever figured out that being informal is a big deal." Transformational leadership theory begins with the leader, flows through every individual employee, and ends with an organizational culture that values every employee, their ideas and creativity, and empowers them in the vision of the future.

(**Note 2**: Beth Williams, CEO & Managing Partner, *Forward Focus.*)

Five Leadership Theories and Styles that Affect the Way Your People See You

A recent study by research groups Barna and Leadercast found that only one in every five workers thinks their boss is a good leader. A massive 40% of workers think their boss is bad, and the remaining 40% think they have an average boss at best. Complaints voiced most commonly about leadership include a lack of vision and a leadership style that is over-controlling and manipulative. A third of workers say that poor leadership is the main factor of stress at work.

Leadership theories and styles vary widely, but the fact that almost two-thirds of workers say that it is only the paycheck that makes them follow their manager cannot be ignored. Poor leadership leads directly to a *disgruntled workforce, decreasing productivity*, and *higher costs as staff turnover skyrockets*. When considering business strategy, leadership theories and styles should be high on the list of things that an organization must get right. But how do these shape up in your organization today, and how would your leaders and employees benefit from a different approach?

1. The natural leader.

The first theory is that leaders are born and not made. This leadership theory has its foundations in history when aristocracy were the natural leaders of people. Often these led by either fear or motivational style but certainly because of the greater education and knowledge of the leader. There may be some truth in the fact that natural leaders appear when the chips are down, but natural leaders from ancient religious figures to Churchill, Eisenhower, and John F. Kennedy all benefited from *a higher level of understanding and access to information than those they led.*

2. Leadership by participation.

Those who lead by participation involve others in the process of decision making. This will include peers, subordinates, superiors, and stakeholders. Highest levels of participation occur when all decisions are made by the team. However, the leader may first sell his or her ideas to team members or describe objectives and encourage the discovery of solutions. This approach helps the leader to empower his or her people, embedding commitment, and encouraging a more collaborative workplace.

3. Leadership by reward/punishment.

Among theories and styles of leadership, this is perhaps one of the most controversial. The premise is that people are motivated to perform either by reward for good performance or punishment for bad. This is most akin to authoritative-style leadership in which people understand the chain of command and react to orders handed to them. This transactional leadership style gives the manager full control and is most commonly portrayed as managers rather than leaders.

4. Motivational leadership.

Leadership by motivation also called transformational leadership is seen when the leader inspires people to follow. This requires vision and passion with the leader's own enthusiasm and energy reflected by that of his or her people. *This type of leader cares about the people for whom he or she has responsibility and is a constant advocate of the future vision.* He or she is likely to be a good negotiator and benefits from high emotional intelligence. Motivational leadership requires the leader to be highly visible, *empathetic*, committed, and visionary. Their concerns are balanced between the well-being of their people and the progress of the project. However, motivational leaders thrive on challenge and so, for this type of leader, frustration will set in when working at an organization that wishes to remain unchanged.

5. Contingency leadership.

The last of these five leadership theories and styles is one of the most difficult to execute effectively. Leadership by contingency requires a flexible approach that is shaped by circumstance. The leader takes into consideration the abilities of his or her people, the needs of the organization, the demands of the project, and his or her own leadership capabilities. For example, projects that are severely time constricted may require a more controlling approach whereas projects of a more technical nature may require a more participatory style.

(Note 3: Beth Williams, CEO & Managing Partner, *Forward Focus.*)

Key Leadership Role Potential

Identifying the *potential* in our current and future leaders is not an easy task but there are tools at our disposal to assist. Chart 1 below serves as an aid to identify (a) high potential, (b) moderate potential, and (c) limited potential members of our team. This helps to distinguish their readiness for higher levels of responsibility and accountability. The four categories of skills required are for (1) Cross-organizational/enterprise, (2) Executive leadership, (3) Change, and (4) Executive communications. As you consider this model to rank your high potential candidates across the four categories of skills, I developed this visual graphic that adds clarity to the expected behaviors:

1. Cross–organizational/enterprise: Does the potential leader understand how to navigate and maneuver through the intricacies of the

office assistant all the way up to the chief executive?

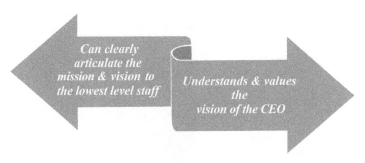

2. <u>Executive Leadership</u>: Will the potential leader represent the organization, internally and externally, in a manner that will portray an image of professionalism, diplomacy, integrity, and trust?

3. <u>Change Leadership</u>: Is the potential leader prepared for the inevitable change that is coming?

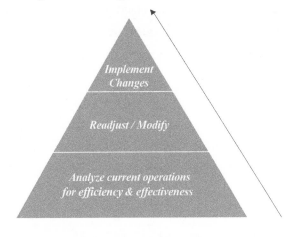

4. <u>Executive Communications:</u> How well does the potential leader communicate and 'connect' with others? Do you and your team understand the three modes of communication?

Chart 1

Modes of Communication

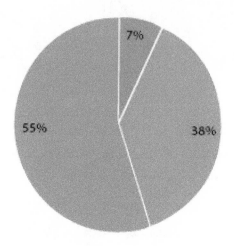

■ Words ■ Tone ■ Body Language

How well they *connect* with others is a combination of <u>three</u> very important determining yet interrelated factors:

- **Words** – the words that we speak only comprise 7% of our total communication and messaging.

- **Tone** – the tone of our voice represents 38% of our total communication and messaging.

- **Body Language** – the non-verbal gestures and postures that are on display send 55% of our messaging—what we think, how we react, and the overall message that we present to others.

Key Leadership Role Potential

Identifying the *potential* in our current and future leaders is not an easy task, but there are tools at our disposal to assist. Chart 2 below serves as an aid to identify high potential, moderate potential, and limited potential members on our team and whether or not they may be ready to accept higher levels of responsibility and accountability. The four categories of skills required are (1) Cross-organizational/enterprise, (2) Executive leadership, (3) Change, and (4) Executive communications. As you consider this model to evaluate your high, moderate, and limited potential candidates across the four categories of skills, analyze each category carefully to determine readiness and likelihood for success.

Chart 2. Key Leadership Role Potential

Cross-organizational / Enterprise leadership	Executive leadership	Change leadership	Executive communications
High Potential			
- Consistently puts interest of the "whole" ahead of own organizational interest - Defaults to cross-organizational team approach to considering issues - Able to assume other organizational perspectives in formulating plans and making decisions - Anticipates 2nd/3rd order effects and	- Leadership focuses on the group's activity rather than own role as the leader - Articulates strategy/vision, then empowers/delegates to execute - Coaches and develops staff and peers, supporting rather than directing - Leads through influence in addition to positional authority	- Excels in dealing with ambiguity **and** in leading teams through ambiguity - Achieves outstanding results while lifting up the team - Manages stress effectively (both personal and organizational) - Responds calmly and decisively to set-backs - Makes timely decisions with information	- Grounds communications in language and framing that demonstrates understanding of audience's perspectives and prerogatives - Communicates confidently and skillfully with internal and external audiences at highest level - Demonstrates openness and sensitivity to diverse perspectives

interdepen-dencies

- Initiates and leads collaborative approaches to cross-organizational issues

- Is very comfortable leading outside own areas of expertise

available

- Promptly and productively addresses conflict and has difficult conversations

- Inspires and engenders continuous learning

- Drives two-way communication / dialogue

Moderate Potential

- Participates collegially in cross-organizational settings but less likely the initial approach

- Listens to diverse perspectives and may act on/incorporate

- Compromises to achieve cross-organizational goals, but rarely initiates compromise solution

- Understands $2^{nd}/3^{rd}$ order effects and interdependencies when presented

- Generally avoids focusing attention on self as the leader

- Consults with staff but does most of the decision-making

- Tends to direct rather than coach

-Intervenes/ "rescues" when problems arise, sometimes too quickly

- Comfortable leading in areas of own expertise, only somewhat comfortable in other areas

- Leadership may rely on positional expertise

- Personally comfortable with ambiguity, but may not account for its effect on group

- Achieves desired results, sometimes to the detriment of the team

- Generally manages stress well

- Generally handles set-backs productively

- Hesitates to make decisions with limited information

- Generally confronts difficult issues, but may hesitate or have difficulty in approach

- Communicates clearly and succinctly to various audiences

- Demonstrates command of material; responds effectively to questions but may not anticipate issues in audience's perspective

- Demonstrates expertise in own knowledge, but may have difficulty conveying that in the language of the audience

- Encourages two-way communication / dialogue

- Emphasizes individual organizational interests; has a zero-sum game mindset	- Often acts and behaves in self-oriented ways	- Struggles to deal with ambiguity	- Uses jargon and/or speaks at a level of detail inappropriate to audience
- Struggles to understand $2^{nd}/3^{rd}$ order effects and interdepen-dencies	- Directive in taskings	- Struggles to achieve results without recognizing effects on others/the team	- Struggles to respond to challenges to perspective or position
- Advocates for own solutions and/or solutions in own interest over enterprise interest	- Struggles to accept input/ideas from others, particularly if quite different from own	- Struggles to maintain composure and effectiveness under stress	- Presents in a manner that is self-oriented
	- Steps in and takes charge as soon as an issue arises	- Resists change (as a default)	- Daunted by audience
	- Struggles to lead when not in his area of expertise	- Blames others for set-backs	
		- Struggles to make/revisits decisions	
		- Shies away from difficult issues or addresses with heavy hand	
		- Focuses on "who did it" versus "lessons learned"	

(**Note 5:** Department of Defense model)

Final Thoughts

Those who cultivate and develop the skill of listening make good team players because they're better able to understand other people's opinions and positions. The Scriptures teach us, *"A wise man will hear and increase learning, And a man of understanding will attain wise counsel"* (Proverbs 1:5, New King James Version).

As leaders celebrate the *potential* in others, the quicker they grow, develop, and mature. My personal journey as a manager and leader modeled, in part, how my own potential was celebrated early in my career by many supervisors and mentors who were instrumental in my success. Mr. Jack Welch led a globally-recognized Fortune 100 firm and increased the company's value by 4,000% during his 20-year tenure as CEO based upon eleven leadership style axiom's. The number one axiom was his way of *celebrating* the potential in every employee by sharing great ideas. While Barna and Leadercast report that 40% of workers think their boss is bad and another 40% think their boss is average at best, one of the top five reasons is because of a lack of leadership by 'participation.' Let's celebrate the potential that lies within the members of our respective teams. See if it works! That's my challenge to you.

A willingness to learn—to try new things and develop new approaches to life—is a *requirement* for anyone who wants to succeed in life. *"If ye be willing and obedient, ye shall eat the good of the land"* (Isaiah 1:19, King James Version).

STUDY QUESTIONS & DISCUSSION

1. How do you *evaluate* the potential in others?

_____

_____

_____

_____

_____

2. What steps will you take to help others reach *their* full potential?

_____

_____

_____

_____

_____

3. Identify three areas of growth that you need in order to *position others* for success.

_____

_____

_____

_____

4. Are you *prepared* and *equipped* to help others grow?

_____

_____

_____

_____

_____

5. Does your current *leadership style* require any modification to effectively lead others?

_____

_____

_____

_____

_____

PART TWO:

the GOAL of Servant Leadership: *Inspiring Others*

"All scripture is given by inspiration of God, and is profitable for doctrine, for reproof, for correction, for instruction in righteousness."
—2 Timothy 3:16 (King James Version)

CHAPTER FOUR

Influence and Impact

"I wanted to show some appreciation for the people who have worked for me and been responsible, to a great length, for the success of the company."

—Lee Schoenberr, Owner of FloraCraft

"Today the Lord your God has commanded you to obey all these decrees and regulations. So be careful to obey them wholeheartedly."

—Deuteronomy 26:16 (New Living Translation)

T HIS IS A BRIEF STORY OF SUPPORT from my favorite teacher from elementary, middle, and high school. Her name is Mrs. Adkins. She was my eleventh grade English teacher at Armstrong High School in my hometown of Richmond, Virginia. One day in class during the first semester of my junior year, Mrs. Adkins' inspirational message of support, encouragement, and advocacy impacted and influenced my life. It was a memorable action on her part that I continue to pay forward as often as I can. It literally changed my life.

Immediately following my dad's retirement from the U.S. Marine Corps after a twenty-year career as an enlisted soldier and commissioned junior officer, my family relocated from Virginia Beach to return home to Richmond. My family and I were accustomed to frequent moves because of dad's occupation. As a young boy, these moves were not very disruptive and I was able to handle the change in environment, neighborhoods, and schools alongside my mom and younger brother, Eric. However, I noticed a shift in emotions as I transitioned into middle and high school. For the first time, as I was suddenly uprooted from a familiar and comfortable surrounding, it mattered!

I attended Floyd E. Kellam High School in Virginia Beach as a freshman and sophomore. During these two phenomenally fun and exciting years of growth, development, maturing, dating, sports, and new friendships, I was excelling academically and athletically. I earned positions on the junior varsity (JV) wrestling and football teams. I wrestled at the 105-pound weight class and started on the football team as one of the three wide receivers. I wore number '88' as I attempted to emulate my favorite professional football player at the time—Lynn Swann of the Pittsburgh Steelers. Our school colors at Kellum were black and gold, just like the Steelers. Our JV wrestling and football teams were competitive and the coaching staff were excellent. I knew I wanted to continue to compete and represent my school. I and my teammates were learning valuable life skills that would sustain us through high school, prepare us for college, and ultimately into the workplace.

At the conclusion of my sophomore year, Dad officially retired during a beautiful military ceremony in Norfolk, Virginia, at the Naval Air Station on a sunny afternoon. Soon, thereafter, he notified our family during one of our weekly meetings that we would be moving back home to Richmond. While I understood and cherished the thought of being in the daily company of my grandparents, aunts, uncles, and cousins, I was devastated by the timing. Leaving my neighborhood and high school friends was heartfelt. Nevertheless, I respected Dad's decision and we spent many days that summer packing and preparing to relocate. Saying goodbye was hard. Tears did flow.

The following school year came quickly. During the month of August, leading up to the start of the new semester in September, Dad enrolled me into Armstrong High School located on the east end of the city in an area known as 'Church Hill.' Under the leadership of Dr. Lucille Brown, Principal, I had a wonderful experience at this school even though my start was a bit rocky. Having a desire to continue my success on the athletic field, I attended tryouts for the varsity basketball team. Although I did not earn a position on the basketball team at Kellam High School in Virginia Beach, I did play a lot on the area playgrounds and was competitive enough to play on an organized team—so I thought. I was an all-star in little league as well as at the middle school levels. As a young sixteen-year-old, I was not aware that the varsity basketball team at Armstrong had already started their practice sessions, that the coaching staff was already familiar with their team of players, and that since the official season begins in October each year, the roster had already been selected. I learned this much later as I inquired about the selection process. However, tryouts were held but only as a formality to see what talent may be available for the following season. I did not earn a position on the varsity basketball team. I and three others were notified by the coaching staff in a most embarrassing way. They posted our names on a chart in the locker room for everyone to see.

During our English 101 class, Mrs. Adkins noticed a change in my demeanor and posture. In her eyes, I was one of her students who excelled in the subject matter, was always in good spirits, and exhibited a mild-mannered disposition. When she saw a different version of Kevin Johnson, she inquired. I informed her that I did not earn a position on the varsity basketball team and how I felt as a result. While she stated that she understood how this may make me feel, she offered a potential solution to ease the pain. Mrs. Adkins has mentioned several times in the past that I was an excellent speaker and a model student. She recommended that I talk to the varsity basketball coach about announcing the games during the upcoming season. This would avail the opportunity to introduce the players, lead the play-by-play action on the court from behind the microphone so that hundreds of spectators could hear my voice. It sounded like a great idea, so I did. The coach said yes! The previous announcer graduated the year prior and the position was vacant. [I discovered later that Mrs. Adkins was well aware of the situation and had lobbied on my behalf!] It was a great season. During this same time, Mrs. Adkins also suggested that I have the same conversation with the varsity football coach. I could potentially become the football announcer from the much larger football stadium where thousands of spectators, not just hundreds, would hear my voice during our home games at half time, for homecoming, and the like. I did. The football coach said yes! It was during these experiences as a junior and senior at Armstrong that I discovered my voice. That led to speaking assignments and helped to enhance my career. I've been speaking publicly ever since.

Mrs. Adkins' kind display of support changed my life in the following ways:

    ✓ I discovered that I am responsible to help others in their time of need.

✓ I was born with a specific purpose (mission) that aligns with God's plan (vision) for my life.

✓ Choices are long-lasting and life-changing. Let's give others within our sphere of influence opportunities to choose their next steps over and beyond their limited options.

The Story of the Southern Poverty Law Center

The Southern Poverty Law Center (SPLC) was founded in 1971 to ensure that the promise of the civil rights movement became a reality for all. By the late 1960s, the civil rights movement had ushered in the promise of racial equality as new federal laws and decisions by the U.S. Supreme Court ended Jim Crow segregation. But resistance was strong, and these laws had not yet brought the fundamental changes needed in the South. African Americans were still excluded from good jobs, decent housing, public office, a quality education, and a range of other opportunities. There were few places for the disenfranchised and the poor to turn to for justice. Enthusiasm for the civil rights movement had waned, and few lawyers in the South were willing to take controversial cases to test new civil rights laws.

> *"Practice and work hard on these things; be absorbed in them [completely occupied in your ministry], so that your progress will be evident to all."*
> 1 Timothy 4:15
> (Amplified Version)

Alabama lawyer and businessman Morris Dees sympathized with the plight of the poor and the powerless. The son of an Alabama farmer, he had witnessed firsthand the devastating consequences of bigotry and racial injustice. Dees decided to sell his successful book publishing business to start a civil rights law practice that would provide a voice for the disenfranchised.

"I had made up my mind," Dees wrote in his autobiography, *A Season for Justice. "I would sell the company as soon as possible and specialize in civil rights law. All the things in my life that had brought me to this point, all the pulls and tugs of my conscience, found a singular peace. It did not matter what my neighbors would think, or the judges, the bankers, or even my relatives."* His decision led to the founding of the Southern Poverty Law Center.

Dees joined forces with another young Montgomery lawyer, Joe Levin. They took pro bono cases few others were willing to pursue, the outcome of which had far-reaching effects. Some of their early lawsuits resulted in the desegregation of recreational facilities, the reapportionment of the Alabama Legislature, the integration of the Alabama state trooper force, and reforms in the state prison system. The lawyers formally incorporated the SPLC in 1971, and civil rights activist Julian Bond was named the first president. Dees and Levin began seeking nationwide support for their work. People from across the country responded with generosity, establishing a sound financial base for the new organization.

In the decades since its founding, the SPLC shut down some of the nation's most violent white supremacist groups by winning crushing, multi-million-dollar jury verdicts on behalf of their victims. It dismantled vestiges of Jim Crow; reformed juvenile justice practices; shattered barriers to equality for women, children, the LGBT community and the disabled; protected low-wage immigrant workers from exploitation; and much more. In the 1980s, the SPLC began monitoring white supremacist activity amid a resurgence of the Klan and today its Intelligence Project is internationally known for tracking and exposing a wide variety of hate and extremist organizations throughout the United States. In the early 1990s, the SPLC launched its pioneering Teaching Tolerance program to provide educators with free, anti-bias classroom resources such as classroom documentaries and lesson plans. Today, it reaches millions of school children with award-winning materials that teach them to respect others and help educators create inclusive, equitable school environments.

As the country has grown increasingly diverse, their work has only become more vital. Our history is evidence of an unwavering resolve to promote and protect our nation's most cherished ideals by standing up for those who have no other champions.

SPLC is a tax-exempt, charitable organization incorporated in 1971 under section 501(c) (3) of the Internal Revenue Code. All contributions, grants, and bequests are tax-deductible. Their tax identification number is 63-0598743. Their work is supported primarily through donor contributions. They do not receive or use government funds. During fiscal year 2016, approximately 68% of total expenses were spent on program services. At the end of fiscal year 2016, their endowment—a special, board-designated fund established to support our future work—stood at $319.3 million.

Leadership with others in mind. SPLC is dedicated to fighting hate and bigotry and to seeking justice for the most vulnerable members of our society. Using litigation, education, and other forms of advocacy, the SPLC works toward the day when the ideals of equal justice and equal opportunity will be a reality. Amongst their multiple life-changing initiatives to enhance the quality of life for others who cannot advocate for themselves, children's rights and economic justice are highlighted below.

Children's Rights

Many vulnerable children across the Deep South of the U.S. are being denied access to a quality public education and the mental health services they need. At the same time, thousands are being pushed out of the classroom and into the juvenile justice system because of discipline policies that punish them severely for minor misbehavior. Alabama, Florida, Georgia, Mississippi, and Louisiana all rank at or near the bottom of the country in terms of poverty, education, health care, and other indicators of children's well-being. Children of color and those with disabilities or mental health conditions are the ones who are harmed the most by these failures particularly as states slash funding for education and social services. We must do better. This is why SPLC is working across the region *using litigation, grassroots organizing, and advocacy* to ensure that every child has an equal opportunity. SPLC is currently focusing on three priorities:

- **Stopping the "school-to-prison pipeline"**

SPLC is working to eliminate exclusionary policies—unnecessary suspensions and expulsions, and school-based arrests of children—that cut short a child's education and increase the likelihood of incarceration.

- **Ensuring equal access to education**

SPLC is working to ensure educational equity for children in poverty and those with disabilities particularly as states transform the educational landscape by allowing charter schools and by shifting public resources to private schools.

- **Ensuring access to mental health services**

SPLC is working to improve access to effective, community-based mental health services and to reduce the over-reliance on institutionalized care that warehouses children without providing the services they need.

There have been many successes in recent years. In Mobile, Alabama, their lawsuit against the school district has resulted in a 75 percent reduction in school days lost to suspension. In New Orleans, they reached a landmark agreement to ensure that children with disabilities have access and proper services in the city's system of charter schools. In Meridian, Mississippi, their investigation sparked a Department of Justice lawsuit that stopped the routine arrest and jailing of children—disproportionately African American—for minor, noncriminal school infractions.

Despite the progress, there is much work still, but they remain steadfast in their commitment to ensuring equality, fairness, and opportunity for all children.

Economic Justice

Poor people in America today are not only facing an economic gap, they're also facing a justice gap. Too often, they're exploited and abused simply for being poor. They're victimized by predatory lenders who trap them in a cycle of debt and rob them and their communities of scant resources. They're denied access to the social safety net by politicians who stigmatize low-income workers and blame them for our country's problems. They're exploited and imprisoned by local governments that target impoverished communities for revenue-generating traffic fines and by companies that seek to profit by charging fees for improper but court-ordered "services" like payment plans.

For more than forty years, SPLC has represented the most vulnerable people in society, often those living in poverty who cannot afford to mount legal challenges to the injustices they faced. Today, their Economic Justice Project is fighting back against deeply ingrained policies and practices that exploit or punish the poor simply because of their economic status. Their work has a national reach but is primarily focused on the Deep South. SPLC is currently focused on three primary areas:

1. Reforming policies that trap the poor in a cycle of court debt.

SPLC wants to abolish the modern-day debtors' prisons prevalent in the Deep South and stop the use of "offender-funded" services such as private, so-called "probation" companies that use the power of the justice system to extort payments from the poor.

2. Protecting low-income consumers from predatory practices.

SPLC is helping lead the charge to protect consumers in Alabama from payday and title lenders that prey upon low-income communities and trap the poor in a cycle of debt. They are educating the public and supporting a national effort to create strong consumer safeguards to rein in this rapacious industry.

3. Protecting the safety net for the poor.

SPLC is working to ensure that the poor are not denied access to the social safety net. In Tennessee, for example, they filed suit when officials erected barriers to keep many residents from obtaining health care coverage under the state's Medicaid program. Their suit led to a settlement that has helped over 20,000 people get much-needed answers about their health care coverage.

SPLC is committed to ensuring that the most vulnerable in our society are treated with fairness and dignity.

I periodically read about the SPLC advocacy efforts as teaching moments in leadership, good and bad. One of their most recent and emotion-filled lawsuits involved a case in defense of a 3-year-old girl who could not advocate for herself:

S.G. VS. THE DORAL ACADEMY, INC.

After a Florida pre-kindergarten program refused to assist a 3-year-old girl with type 1 diabetes by monitoring her glucose levels, the

SPLC filed a lawsuit on behalf of the child. Reflecting a statewide problem faced by many children with diabetes, the lawsuit describes how the program violated the Americans with Disabilities Act (ADA) by refusing to accommodate the student's needs. The girl—"S.G."—had a glucose sensor and insulin pump attached to her body to manage her sugar level. As a result of the program's refusal to accommodate her needs, S.G.'s glucose levels were unnecessarily and consistently high during school hours, placing her at unreasonable risk of harm. By federal law, her pre-kindergarten program in the Miami suburb of Doral was supposed to accommodate her special needs. Title III of the ADA prohibits discrimination on the basis of disability by private entities open to the public, including nurseries, child-care facilities, and other places of education. A settlement agreement was reached to ensure The Doral Academy Preschool takes steps to ensure it does not discriminate against children with diabetes. It included monitoring students with diabetes, assisting with blood glucose tests, and taking other steps necessary to accommodate their special needs as required by federal and state law. These steps can help prevent diabetic children from suffering harmful—possibly even fatal—complications while at school.

This case was settled on November 24, 2014, in favor of the plaintiffs. I am thankful for the leadership at SPLC for their unwavering efforts and advocacy for others.

Humility

In the Book of Philippians, Paul writes a thank-you note to the believers at Philippi for their help in his hour of need, and he uses the occasion to send along some instruction on Christian unity. His central thought is simple: Only in Christ are real unity and joy possible. With Christ as your model of humility and *service*, you can enjoy oneness of purpose, attitude, goal, and labor—a truth which Paul illustrates from his own life and one the Philippians desperately need to hear.

> *"Therefore if you have any encouragement from being united with Christ, if any comfort from his love, if any common sharing in the Spirit, if any tenderness and compassion, then make my joy complete by being like-minded, having the same love, being one in spirit and of one mind. Do nothing out of selfish ambition or vain conceit. **Rather, in humility value others above yourselves, not looking to your own interests but each of you to the interests of the others.**"*
>
> —Philippians 2:1-4 (New International Version)

Through his teaching, Paul's message focuses on five key characteristics and attributes that are required for servant leadership. They are:

- Love – *Love never fails [it never fades nor ends]...* (1 Corinthians 13:8 – Amplified).

- Oneness – *There is one body, and one Spirit, even as ye are called into one hope of your calling. One Lord, one faith, one baptism, one God and Father of all, who is above all, and through all, and in you all* (Ephesians 4:4-6 – King James Version).

- Selflessness – *When people live so that they please the LORD, even their enemies will make peace with them* (Proverbs 16:7 – New Century Version).

- Value others – The Golden Rule

- Prioritize the interest of others through your actions – *Dear friends, let us continue to love one another, for love comes from God. Anyone who loves is a child of God and knows God. But anyone who does not love does not know God, for God is love. God showed how much he loved us by sending his one and only Son into the world so that we might have eternal life through him. This is real love—not that we loved God, but that he loved us and sent his Son as a sacrifice to take away our sins. Dear friends, since God loved us that much, we surely ought to love each other* (1 John 4:7-11 – New Living Translation).

Rather than incessantly talk and "hog" every conversation, we who are leaders must learn to make room for the gifts that lay resident in other people. Their talents and gifts are just as vital and important as ours.

Humility, then, incorporates these five essential characteristics of GREAT leaders. Apply, practice, and live by these principles. Those who are entrusted to follow you will be thrilled to fulfill their responsibilities as team players and contributors to the overall mission and vision that you set for your organization, church, or business.

Zero Tolerance

On February 17, 2019, columnist Jena McGregor penned an article "CEOs in an Era of Zero Tolerance" that reflects both the current state of affairs with our senior leaders and the swinging of the pendulum regarding ethics and integrity—two of the highest characteristics. It centers on former REI Chief Executive Officer Jerry Stritzke, who resigned his position because of a "perceived conflict of interest." This insightful piece reminds all leaders that questionable behavior

> "Don't do anything only to get ahead. Don't do it because you are proud. Instead, be humble. Value others more than yourselves."
> Philippians 2:3
> (New International Readers Version)

must be reported to the board especially in today's era of emphasis on executive integrity and zero tolerance for misbehavior.

Outdoor apparel and gear retailer REI acknowledged the resignation of their CEO on February 14, 2019, after a board investigation found that the relationship between him and "the leader of another organization in the outdoor industry" had not been disclosed. Although the inquiry found that no financial misconduct resulted from the relationship, "the facts led to a perceived conflict of interest," board chairman Steve Hooper wrote in a letter to employees "which he should have disclosed under the REI conflict of interest policy, which requires every REI executive to model the highest standard of conduct."

Further, Stritzke's resignation comes about seven months after Intel chief executive Brian Krzanich stepped down for violating a "non-fraternization" policy by having a consensual relationship with another employee. The CEOs of two other tech firms, Rambus and Texas Instruments, also departed last summer after unspecified conduct issues that either "fell short of the company's standards" or violated the code of conduct via personal behavior inconsistent with "our ethics and values." In December, the CEO of electronics component supplier Kemet departed following an investigation of "a consensual personal relationship."

Some evidence appears to show an uptick in how much boards are cracking down on executive's conduct violations. A study by the PwC consulting arm Strategy& in 2017 found that although the number of CEOs kicked out for ethical lapses is small (just 18 among the world's 2,500 largest public companies in 2016), they grew from 3.9 percent of all CEO handoffs between 2007 and 2011 to 5.3 percent from 2012 to 2016, a 36 percent increase.

Following the departure of the Intel CEO, employment lawyer Valerie Hoffman with Seyfarth Shaw wrote that public company boards of directors now "have an extraordinary low tolerance for bad or non-compliant behavior by CEOs, even CEOs who are otherwise very successful. There has been a sea of change in this in the last 18 months."

(**Note 1:** *The Washington Post*, Section G (Metro) by Jena McGregor, February 17, 2019.)

Further, on November 16, 2011, Ed O'Keefe shared his analysis and rehearsal in an article titled "Federal Workers Get Gloomier about Jobs: Survey Finds Decline in Satisfaction for the First Time in 4 Years." In part, his work concludes that satisfaction among federal workers is down for the first time in four years, according to an annual survey of government agencies that ranks attitudes about everything from agency leaders to workplace culture. Concerns about pay, leadership, and department's missions are the main factors behind the growing gloom. Agency heads and the rank in file agree that President Obama's decision to freeze salaries for two years and Republican efforts to cut government programs are contributing to the unease in federal offices. "We're learning to do more with less," said John Reynolds, a management analyst with the Environmental Protection Agency. "But that's consistent across the country, not just in government."

(**Note 2**: *The Washington Post*, Section A, November 16, 2011 (front page)

Final Thoughts

If you're serious about being successful, then you'll have to give your full attention to whatever God has called you to do. Your task must have your full consideration, your undivided attention, and your mental and spiritual concentration. Distractions are not allowed.

Take the time to impact and influence the lives of others. That is precisely how we pay forward our thanks to those who helped us along the way.

STUDY QUESTIONS & DISCUSSION

1. As a mentor, do you follow up regularly to evaluate progress? If not, why?

_____

_____

_____

_____

_____

2. As a leader, you attract who you are, not who you want. What are your thoughts about this?

_____

_____

_____

_____

_____

3. Why aren't force, intimidation, or manipulation effective leadership principles?

_____

_____

_____

_____

_____

4. Mutual respect is a proven core leadership value. Do you respect those whom you are entrusted to lead?

_____

_____

_____

_____

_____

5. Describe your ideal win-win scenario with your team.

_____

_____

_____

_____

_____

CHAPTER FIVE

A Leader Who Inspires

"That divisiveness of pitting people against each other all the time has really worn the business community down."

—Jeffrey Sonnenfeld,
President of Chief Executive Leadership Institute (in response to a survey during the "CEO Summit" hosted by the Yale School of Management's Chief Executive Institute in addressing the 45th President of the United States' leadership style)

"Jesus said to him, "You shall love the Lord your God with all your heart, with all your soul, and with all your mind.' This is the first and great commandment. And the second is like it: 'You shall love your neighbor as yourself.'"

—Matthew 22:37-39 (New King James Version)

J ames Sale, an English businessman and the creator of Motivational Maps which operates in fourteen countries, says, "Leadership is difficult to write about and to deliver." One leading theorist, Adrian Furnham, wrote, "The topic of leadership is one of the oldest areas of research in the social sciences, yet one of the most problematic. Because we experience leadership all the time—in our homes, schools, social institutions, and workplaces—our over-familiarity with the subject tends to lead us to believe we know what it is, just as we think we know what education is because we attended school once upon a time."

It was a logical choice for me to attend Virginia Commonwealth University (VCU) to pursue my undergraduate studies immediately following graduation from Armstrong High School. As a youngster who enjoyed the challenges of gainful employment while earning a decent salary since the age of fourteen, I elected to retain my part-time jobs through high school and college. I could enjoy the comforts of home, study locally at a recognized university, and secure tenure on the job that I cherished. As I recall, I applied to four colleges during my senior year of high school and was selected by two. VCU was one of the two. At the time, the VCU student population was approximately 13,000 and growing. This was also during a time when the university was seeking to embrace more diversity within our student body, administration, and faculty. The timing was perfect.

I began taking classes during the summer just before the official beginning of my new adventures on the VCU campus. I was advised that this was contingent upon my official acceptance through demonstration of my acumen and will to succeed. As always, I welcomed this challenge. The three "A's" (one was non-credit) and one "B" that I earned that summer proved my readiness to enter the gates of VCU.

I initially declared the "Pre-Med" major with the hopes and aspirations of becoming a family physician. There were two primary reasons for this. First, as a child, I suffered for many years with asthma:

trouble breathing, persistent coughing, wheezing, and the constant irritability associated with being uncomfortable. I also suffered from hay fever: nonstop sneezing especially during the springtime as the flowers bloom, and living in close proximity to dust. My parents and I made multiple visits to medical facilities, physicians, and medical specialists for the first eleven years of my life. Unable to pinpoint an exact cause, I suffered endlessly through these illnesses. Medications, over-the-counter as well as prescribed, did not work or ease the pain. Removal of my tonsils at age six did not offer a cure. Finally, at the age of eleven years, seven months the symptoms disappeared. I recovered fully with an explanation that I outgrew the illnesses. I was inspired to move on with my life, and I did.

Second, the Medical College of Virginia, an extension of VCU, is a leading university hospital in my hometown. Their research and day-to-day work in the local community was at the forefront of making many, many breakthroughs in the medical field. I admired the professionalism of the entire medical staff as they tried to help my parents and me through the tough times. Even though the physicians and specialists could not offer much relief from illnesses, I still remember how they *inspired* me while seeking helpful remedies.

By the time I entered the first semester of my junior year, I officially declared a "Business" major through the School of Business. At the time, Howard Tuckman was the Dean of the school. He was a man whom I admired, in part because he was approachable and would allow me to come into his office to talk about class assignments. Under his leadership was my Economics 301 professor, Dr. George Coffer. This man was full of energy, humor, and inspiration. His style of teaching economics was fun, intuitive, innovative, and easy to understand. He simplified the often-complicated subject of economics, a social science concerned chiefly with description and analysis of the production, distribution, and consumption of goods and services. Unbeknownst to me at the time, Dr. Coffer displayed four leadership principles during his classes:

- Make sure that all can see that you thoroughly enjoy your work.

- Work hard to simplify what appears to be complex (until you become familiar with the content).

- It's okay to laugh at yourself. Dr. Coffer would tell us jokes about why he would shave at night to avoid that chore each morning. He asked us to please ignore his daily beard shadow.

- Have a real concern for others. Our fulfillment comes from our service toward others.

Dr. Coffer is now VCU's Economics professor emeritus. He's been on the job as a well-respected economics professor for close to forty years. He is still a leader who inspires the current and next generation of leaders—VCU School of Business students—to excel. He is still teaching them not to be overwhelmed by the perceived knowledge needed to learn the skill of leadership. I am rooting for each of these students to implement what is being taught as I did over thirty-five years ago.

How to Engage the Workforce

Leaders are learners. I encourage leaders to read one book each month that will broaden our knowledge and awareness about leadership principles and strategies. In the spirit of the advice that I give to others, not only do I read a book each month on average, but I supplement that reading with several articles on the topics of self-improvement and leadership to remain sharp and competitive in the marketplace. One such recent article is titled, "The First Thing Leaders Need to Do: Leaders Need to Build Community in the Workplace as it is Hard to Trust People You Don't Know," by Jann Freed, Ph.D. It begins with a question: What is the leading cause of death?

a. High blood pressure

b. Inactivity

c. Social isolation

d. High cholesterol

e. Alcohol

f. Obesity

If you answered **c**, you are correct.

The lesson I learned from that question is: Our actions as leaders can perhaps contribute to any of the six possible answers posed through our interactions with those with whom we are entrusted to lead. Unless we take the time to build relationships, exhibit empathy, and show compassion toward others, we are at fault and should be held accountable.

Vivek Murthy, the U.S. Surgeon General from 2014 to 2017, wrote a report that social isolation or loneliness is a more serious health problem than opiates. "Loneliness and weak social connections are associated with a reduction in lifespan similar to that caused by smoking fifteen cigarettes a day and even greater than that associated with obesity." It is connected, he wrote, "with a greater risk of cardiovascular disease, dementia, depression, and anxiety." We live and work in the most technologically connected age in the history of civilization. Yet the rates of loneliness have doubled since the 1980s. Today, more than 40 percent of adults in America report feeling lonely. In England, former Prime Minister Theresa May, in 2018, appointed a minister of Loneliness, saying, "For far too many people, loneliness is the sad reality of modern life."

In his report, Murthy identifies five steps that can help build stronger social relationships. They are:

Building Stronger Relationships

- Evaluate the state of connections: Quality of relationships is more important than quantity.

- Help people understand high-quality relationships: Help people understand the value of strong social connections and how they should be mutually beneficial.

- Make building community an organizational priority: Make sure the organizational culture and policies support the development of trusted social relationships.

- Encourage employees to reach out and help others and to accept the help of others: When feeling lonely, reaching out to help or to accept help can benefit both parties.

- Create opportunities to learn more about your colleagues' personal lives.

Dave Ulrich has been ranked as one of the top business thinkers by several sources and is the author of *The Why of Work*. He finds the concept of "belonging" a critical factor for overcoming social isolation and for creating organizational cultures where people thrive, not just survive. When someone belongs, there is a strong emotional attachment to another person or organization and their personal well-being increases which enhances productivity and performance. When asked how to create a sense of belonging, Ulrich lists four key concepts:

Concept of Belonging

- Belonging requires work and effort. Leaders who are too busy tend to erode belonging. It takes time and effort to invest in building relationships that work.

- Belonging requires making social media more social. Use technology to build connections, not contacts.

- Belonging requires empathy. Leaders need to understand and feel what others are experiencing. This can be done by asking others how you might help them or being aware of their personal circumstances.

- Belonging requires people who are agents for themselves. Leaders can shape personal accountability by helping employees shift their perspective. The questions change from "Do I like my pay, boss, or working conditions?" to "Do I do my best to earn my pay, build a relationship with my boss, or improve working conditions?"

The conclusion of the report by Murthy states, "Leaders must take action now to build the connections that are the foundation of strong companies and strong communities, and that ensures greater health and well-being for all of us."

(**Note 1:** *Training Magazine*, May/June 2019, page 10 by Jann Freed, Ph.D.)

Good Leaders Should Love the People They Lead:
The Typical Day of a Leader—You!

The daily life of a leader is filled with demands and expectations. They derive from three primary sources, but there are others as well. The three primary groups of individuals who lean heavily on leaders for their advice, experience, guidance, acumen, support, and direction are:

- The Boss
- The Peers / colleagues
- The Staff / direct reports

Given the multi-faceted role and responsibility of a leader, there are high expectations that the organization's mission and vision will be upheld because the leader is the 'glue' that keeps everything working together. Maintaining a smooth running engine is commonplace for the leader. Below is an illustration that I use in all of the leadership courses I regularly teach. It's a practice that is applicable to the government, corporations, churches, academia, and the non-profit workforce.

YOU are in the middle and are expected to manage all expectations from those around YOU:

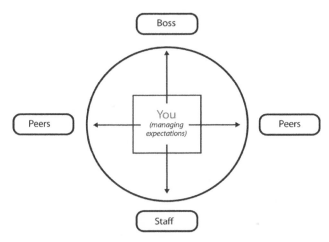

The Boss – This is the person who dependents upon you as the leader. The boss delegates key tasks to you regularly. He relies upon you to deliver briefings in his absence, to attend meetings when he is double-booked; he asks you to lead the weekly staff meeting, assigns you to proofread important documents on his behalf, and periodically calls you into his office to get your advice on delicate topics without advance notice.

The Peers (colleagues) – Your peers call upon you in a time of need to complete a project, to solicit advice, and or to talk about how you would handle a particular situation. Your peers are an integral part of your network and should be a resource to lean upon during a time of crisis as well as when all is well.

The Staff (direct reports) – Your staff values your mentorship and coaching. As their leader, they are counting on your support in assisting them with their upward mobility in the organization. Their performance rating is tied with how well they perform and produce based upon the objectives and elements you drafted. They watch your every move and keep in mind that your verbal, as well as your non-verbal communication, sends a message to them.

The typical day of a leader is a combination of interaction with the boss, your peers, and your staff. Serving as the 'glue' to keep everything flowing is a very high calling and expectation. You are entrusted by many to achieve the desired results. This summarizes why good leadership is so critically important in today's workplace.

Changing Workplace Culture

Experts say one of the most important things companies focused on culture can do is to make sure they send consistent messages about how they handle employee misconduct, whether that involves a high-profile superstar or someone in the trenches.

> *"You almost have to assume that these things are going to become public...at some point. There's an argument it's worse for it to come out later."*
> Amy Bess, employment lawyer with Vedder Price, Washington, DC, about how companies handle misconduct allegations.

During the Fall of 2018, global giant Uber initiated several internal changes under the leadership of CEO Dara Khosrowshahi. At the core of these changes was a push to improve the company's culture. He cas the vision: "Do the right thing. Period," a company mantra and moving beyond a list of "norms" that once included "always be hustling." Prior to his arrival as CEO, Uber fired twenty employees and placed more in training or counseling as the result of a workplace investigation. It also pledged to implement recommendations from a top-to-bottom workplace review. Among other things, Uber has hired a chief diversity officer, invested in new training, and revamped its performance review system.

In his case, this is more than just management pablum; cleaning up Uber's culture will also be essential to reaping the rewards of an initial public offering that has been valued at $120 billion. He has repeatedly acknowledged there is more work to do. "My second year is going to be much more internally focused," he said, "to make sure that we're not only the company we dreamed of being to the world, but most importantly we're that company to all of our employees."

> "People will forget what you said and did, but they will never forget how you made them feel."
>
> Maya Angelou

(**Note 2**: *The Washington Post*, G5, "On Leadership," October 28, 2018, by Jena McGregor)

The average holiday bonus in 2017 among workers who actually got them was about $1,800, according to one survey of accountants. But a floral foam-maker based in Ludington, Michigan, is giving an amount that could make the Grinch smile, announcing a bonus likely to average more than $14,000 per worker. FloraCraft which manufactures, fabricates, and markets foam products—those green or white blocks— told its employees it will be paying $4 million in bonuses. The move comes after a strong year for the business and a tax law that slashed corporate taxes. Schoenherr, eighty-three, who has led the company since 1973 and served as chairman, said he wanted to do something more "meaningful." He typically gives an extra week's pay as a holiday bonus to his workers. But Schoenherr had been thinking for years of making a substantial gift to workers as a way of saying thanks. "I wanted to show some appreciation for the people who have worked for me and been responsible, to a great length, for the success of the company," he said. He decided the time was right in 2018. The tax cut provided a cushion. "The business was reaping the benefits of years of investing in research and development that allowed it to manufacture foam, rather than buy it externally," chief executive Eric Erwin said.

(**Note 3:** *The Washington Post*, G3, "On Leadership," December 23, 2018, by Jena McGregor)

How to Help Ourselves & Others Understand the Purpose in Life

Scott Mann is a former Green Beret who specialized in unconventional, high-impact missions and relationship building. As the founder of Rooftop Leadership and through frequent appearances on TV and syndicated radio programs, he shares many foundational leadership principles that promote growth and development at all levels within an organization. In his featured article, "Understanding Your Purpose in Life, The Epoch Times on Leadership: Leading with Wisdom," January 2019, he begins with three eye-opening thoughts for leaders to consider:

1. We are wired to seek out purpose. We're the most meaning-seeking creatures on the planet; we absolutely crave meaning.

2. Why is purpose so important? Simply put, because we're human.

3. The American warrior will do anything that you ask of them, of their own free will, if they know the answer to one simple question: Why?

He goes on to write that you cannot explain to someone else why they should take action if you don't understand your own purpose, your "why." Simon Sinek was right when he said, "People don't buy what you do; they buy why you do it." But there's a challenge. It's easy to see the sight of our higher purpose in today's transactional society and rat race. Before you know it, we've buried our own purpose, and we're focused on helping someone else achieve theirs. Even if we're making tons of money, we're not necessarily fulfilling that sense of purpose and meaning that we crave and need. There are plenty of miserable rich people, and it's often because their lives lack purpose.

I believe we are creatures of purpose. We are all here to do something bigger than ourselves. We're all here to play a bigger game. Think about it. The happiest, most rewarding moments in your life are when you are achieving a purpose that's bigger than yourself because it begins to satisfy the two biggest questions we ask ourselves: "Who am I?" and "Why am I here?' I also believe that as leaders, we can take time out periodically for introspection. Try this: Go someplace quiet and just reflect for five minutes, asking yourself these questions: "Am I playing the game that I was put here to play? If not, am I playing somebody else's game? Have I lost sight of the game that I'm supposed to be playing?" You don't have to answer what that game is just yet, or what your purpose is—that will come in time. You will know in your **heart** and in your gut if you're playing the game you were meant to play. If you are, then ask yourself: "Am I playing that game as well as I could? Am I as clear on my purpose as I could be?" And if you know deep down in the core of your being that you're not, then be honest with yourself.

This world is starved for authentic, transparent, effective leadership that moves people to action. We need this from you. We need you to be clear on your purpose.

There is a concrete reason some people succeed and others fail. A lack of preparation makes many people ill-equipped for the obstacles they will inevitably face along the way.

"Study and do your best to present yourself to God approved, a workman [tested by trial] who has no reason to be ashamed, accurately

handling and skillfully teaching the word of truth."

—2 Timothy 2:15 (Amplified)

Measuring Leadership Development

Leadership development programs are commonplace; less commonplace is an effective way to measure if they work! Companies are making an effort to determine whether and how leaders and their organizations are benefiting from these programs.

The impact of a toxic executive can be substantial including the loss of star employees and departments that fail to reach business goals. Well-liked but ineffective leaders can be equally damaging, impeding the company's profitability. With so much at stake, organizations are wondering how to gauge the effectiveness of their leadership development programs. Does the coursework result in great leaders, or are these programs nice to have but not essential to high-performing leadership? Here are what five *Training Top 125* companies and a learning technology developer are doing to measure whether often-expensive leadership development programs deliver the desired results:

1. Formal Assessments and Leader Feedback

C&A Industries

Before you can assess if a leadership development program works, you need to define success. "Effective leadership development means empowering our leaders by providing them with the tools they need to lead their group in a direction that meets the overall objectives of the company," says Breanna C. White, project manager at C&A Industries. "Simply put, alignment and execution. If we are effective in our training, leaders can think critically, align their goals with the corporate direction, and execute with confidence, all while needing little guidance to do so. Lastly, effective leadership development means creating a culture that is open to learning; fosters continuous growth through the sharing of ideas; and never stops trying to get better."

To this end, the company uses the DiSC 363 assessment tool to gain an understanding of the top three things their teams need more: more feedback, rallying the troops, and positive workplace. White says, "Training then partners with the manager to design goals aimed at improving the identified areas; these goals then are reassessed after a minimum of six months."

2. Prompt Reflection and Self-Assessment
AlloSource

Employees in leadership development programs are asked to analyze their own progress on a daily basis, says Director of Training and Development Mark Lenahan. In March 2018, AlloSource partnered with Avanoo to announce a new training program for managers. The program begins with a daily email from Avanoo with a link to that day's video. Upon clicking the link, employees are asked to complete a "Check-In" where they rate their ability to focus on the day's lesson. Once they make their choice, the daily video loads, about three minutes in length and consists of a story, a lesson, and an action. Upon viewing the video, employees are taken to the "Action Board" where they can reflect on the lesson or engage in discussions with their colleagues.

3. Ask Direct Reports What They Think
SkillSoft

Learning technology developer Skillsoft values the input of direct reports. Their leadership development program uses feedback from employees to gauge leaders' progress. "Effective leadership development is all about substantive behavioral change," says Senior Vice President of Content Product Management Heidi Abelli. "If leaders do not change their daily behavior and practices as a result of having gone through the development program, then we have not met our objectives. The key is changed daily practices and behaviors that enable the leader to lead a team of individuals more effectively to accomplish business goals and objectives; drive employee engagement and commitment; and create an atmosphere of trust, loyalty, and responsibility within the team."

The team developed a multi-rater assessment containing approximately sixty-five questions that take a leader's direct report about thirty minutes to complete and is administered at least once every three months. The results of the summary report then provide the basis for a personalized learning plan for the leader that emphasizes areas where the leader may still require improvement, whether it is in the area of coaching or providing feedback or driving execution.

4. Measure How Their Department is Doing
SpawGlass

"At SpawGlass, metrics used to measure leader effectiveness look at the department's overall performance," says Team Member Development Manager Charles Mogab. The company has ten operating groups, and all ten leaders have been promoted from within and have attended its leadership programs. Part of observing how whole teams of employees—rather than just the leader—are doing is adapting course material as needed. "Although the core content of both our leadership workshops has remained basically the same over the years, we have modified the courses to reflect changes in our strategic plan, the size of our company, and the changing workforce," says Mogab, noting that the multiple generations in SpawGlass' workforce mean the need for leadership development programs on how best to manage Millennials and how to incorporate coaching techniques. "Continuous change and continuous improvement is what keeps our leadership development workshops fresh and impactful."

5. Measure the Trajectory of the Leader's Career

The Guardian Life Insurance Company

How long leaders stay with your organization and how far they go in their career while there can be other good measures of leadership development success. At the Guardian Life Insurance Company, measuring the success of leadership development includes tracking the retention and mobility of participants within the enterprise. "We use a variety of measurement strategies, depending on the length and intensity of the program. For shorter programs, such as individual workshops, we focus on Net Promoter Score (NPS) and Value for Time Spent, along with pre- and post-confidence self-assessments. For longer, more robust programs, we measure retention of talent advancement and mobility of talent and business impact," says head of Learning and Career Development Gail Kelman. For instance, Guardian has measured that for its Emerging Leader Development Program, it has retained 98 percent of graduates since the program's inception three years ago. Some 95 percent of graduates indicate an increase in their network; 70 percent indicate an increase in their knowledge of the businesses that represent the enterprise, and 55 percent of graduates have been promoted or moved on to other roles within the organization.

"In addition, many of our programs have business-related projects embedded within the coursework," Kelman says. "We measure the investment, implementation, and results of those projects. For example, our Commercial and Government Markets organization recently invested $350,000 to pilot one project, which leverages artificial intelligence to create an exceptionally engaging client experience."

(**Note 4:** *Training* Magazine, May/June 2019, page 26, by Margery Weinstein)

Final Thoughts

Chris Erickson a combat veteran and former Green Beret says, "It's easy to be a happy, motivated member of a team when everything is sunshine, lollipops, and rainbows. It's when it takes real effort to make the best of the given circumstances that you see what people are made of at the cellular level." How true.

In my journey to inspire, motivate, and lead people in the workplace, both government and corporate, and in the church, I stand firm on these two truths, both extracted from the Book of Proverbs 3:13-14 and 21:25, respectively:

1) Search high and low for people who read books, listen to teaching tapes, and attend seminars to learn how to perform their responsibilities and improve their skills. Choose those who strive for excellence in the way they live, where they live, and how they dress.

2) You can send people to school, educate them, and even pay for them to fly halfway around the world to learn new and better techniques, but if they don't possess the inner drive to become better and more professional, it doesn't matter how much time or money you throw at them; it's all a waste unless they have desire.

Inspiring others begins with the *inspiration* that lies within us as leaders. While leadership is difficult to write about and deliver, it is achievable with the right motives. As the glue that keeps our organizations intact, be mindful of your purpose, destiny, goals, dreams, and aspirations. They will keep you focused on the task-at-hand which is to love the people whom you are entrusted to lead. The *inspiration* that comes from the behaviors, mannerisms, and attitudes of the leader ultimately saturates the organization that we lead. Will that be you?

STUDY QUESTIONS & DISCUSSION

1. What leadership style do you portray that causes others to want to follow?

_____

_____

_____

_____

_____

2. What great leader inspired you toward achieving your dreams, goals, and aspirations?

_____

_____

_____

_____

_____

3. How do you respond to a person who is not motivated to fulfill his responsibilities?

_____

_____

_____

_____

_____

4. Why do you believe it takes inspiration and a desire to become a good leader?

_____

_____

_____

_____

_____

5. Have you experienced working with people who do not believe they have the knowledge to be a good leader? If so, how did you help them overcome their fear?

_____

_____

_____

_____

_____

CHAPTER SIX

The Compassionate Leader

"Leaders who don't listen will eventually be surrounded by people who have nothing to say."

—Andy Stanley

"You must each decide in your heart how much to give. And don't give reluctantly or in response to pressure. 'For God loves a person who gives cheerfully.'"

—2 Corinthians 9:7 (New Living Translation)

"*I HAVE AN INNER URGE TO SERVE MANKIND*," said Reverend Dr. Martin Luther King, Jr. as he was ordained into the ministry at age nineteen. A follower and frequent listener to Dr. King's speeches and sermons, my childhood church bears the exact same name as the church he served in his early years. His church was in Atlanta, Georgia; mine in Richmond, Virginia. The church's name, Ebenezer Baptist Church, reminds me of Dr. King's compassion for all people as he served both inside and outside of the confines of his local church. The name is a reminder to me to enter into servanthood and deliberately look for ways to help people discover their goals and dreams.

My journey toward leadership began at Ebenezer Baptist Church. During my formative years as a child, I still remember entering the church building on Sunday mornings with my parents to attend Sunday school and my Cub Scout meetings. I climbed up the two steps leading into the church with my left hand grasping my mom's right hand and my right hand firmly gripped to my dad's left hand. I always wore a bow or necktie to accompany my outfit for the occasion. After entering into the fellowship hall, I was greeted by Mrs. Flowers my Sunday school and music teacher. She led our class time of singing and study followed by my weekly piano lesson plan. It was a joy and honor to learn from a dynamic teacher whose gifts were leading the children of the church while filling us with confidence and excitement. At the conclusion of one hour with Mrs. Flowers, my male classmates and I proceeded to our Cub Scout meeting and activities with Deacon Ross. He resembled a 'gentle giant,' a large kindhearted man whose sole interest was to ensure that the young boys in the church were courteous, obedient, respectful, and ready for training to be the next generation of leaders. He accomplished these goals through his character. I watched, listened, and learned. These moments marked the beginnings of my leadership adventures.

Mrs. Flowers and Deacon Ross exemplified a genuine and caring demeanor that still resonates with me. It's a constant reminder that when leaders pour into the lives of others, we make a big impact, so do it with compassion.

With All My Heart

A compassionate leader is one who leads others "*with all my heart*." In Deuteronomy 6:5, God tells His people that they must love the Lord their God with all their heart, soul, and strength. Let us look at this word *heart*:

Heart (*lēb* or *lēbāb* in the Hebrew)

Our expressions "*with all my heart*," "*my heart wasn't in it*," "*lionhearted*," "*heartless*," and many more show how similar English and Hebrew are in usage of the word *heart*. The Hebrews used *heart* on a broader scale than we do. Theologians often divide man's personality into intellect, sensibility (emotion), and will. The Old Testament uses *lēb* to express all three of these, especially, as in English, emotion.

Intellect (mind). Sometimes *heart* is translated *mind.* Often the context determines when this aspect of heart is emphasized. For example, Proverbs 12:11 tells us that "he that followeth vain *persons* is void of understanding [*lēb*]."

Sensibility (emotion). *Lēb* expresses the whole gamut of emotions, both negative and positive. Second Samuel 17:10 speaks of the "heart of a lion" from bravery. Hannah's heart rejoiced (1 Samuel 2:1). "Jacob's heart fainted" with rapture when he found out that Joseph was still alive (Genesis 45:26). God Himself "was grieved...at His heart" because of man's wickedness (Genesis 6:6). When David says "my heart faileth me" (Psalm 40:12), he is not referring to physical "heart failure"; he is oppressed by the innumerable evils opposing him and fearful of his own iniquities overtaking him.

Will. As the seat of being, the heart makes decisions that express a person's will. For example, Moses explained that he was following the Lord's dictates in all his works, and he had "not *done them* of mine own mind" (literally, "*from my heart*," Numbers 16:28).

(**Note 1**: The Holy Bible, The New Open Bible Study Edition (King James Version), Thomas Nelson Publishers ©1990.)

Compassion for the Current State

I am determined that the results from a 2013 survey by Barna Group titled, "Leadership, Calling and Career," is required reading for all leaders in government, corporations, academia, non-profit organizations, and churches. The report opens with an appropriate commentary that the state of selected world leaders is perceived by observers in every nation. It reads in part:

"No matter what's happening around the world, leadership takes center stage. Kim Jong Un is leading his nation to the brink of war. A group of Senators is directing their Senate compatriots to adopt new policies about illegal immigration. People speculate where the new Pope and the new Archbishop of Canterbury will take their respective churches. On a daily basis, the cable news talking heads either applaud or excoriate the leadership of President Obama. Concern over leadership is, it seems, everywhere in church and culture. But that also makes it difficult to define. Leadership is one of those 'if you see it, you know it' kind of qualities. It's something Americans clearly value, all the way from their immediate employer to their minister to their president. And, according to a new survey conducted by the Barna Group, more than eight in ten (82%) Christian adults believe the United States is facing a crisis of leadership because there aren't enough leaders. What do people value in a leader? What is the Christian perspective of leadership? And is the younger generation looking for a different type of leader?"

> "If my people understand me, I'll get their attention. If my people trust me, I'll get their action."
>
> Cavett Roberts

The study on which this report is based included online surveys with 1,116 adults who were randomly chosen from the United States who also consider themselves Christian. The study was conducted between June 5 and June 11, 2012, using the web-enabled KnowledgePanel®, a probability-based panel designed to be representative of the U.S. population, operated by Knowledge Networks. The research was commissioned by Brad Lomenick, who is the author of a book on leadership called, *Catalyst Leader.* The research was directed and analyzed by David Kinnaman, president of Barna Group. For the purposes of this research, the following short descriptions were given to respondents on ten leadership characteristics:

- Courage – being willing to take risks
- Vision – knowing where you are going
- Competence – being good at what you do
- Humility – giving credit to others
- Collaboration – working well with others
- Passion for God – loving God more than anything else
- Integrity – doing the right thing
- Authenticity – being truthful and reliable
- Purpose – being made for or "called" to the job
- Discipline – the ability to stay focused and get things done

The Traits that Make a Leader

What's the most important quality in a leader? The primary answer is "integrity." More than half (64%) of Christians say integrity is one of the most important traits a leader must-have. Other traits Christians say are important include authenticity (40% listed this as a vital characteristic) and discipline (38%). In fact, Christian adults chose all three of these qualities above "passion for God"—less than one-third (31%) listed that as a necessary trait. The traits Christian adults were least likely to select as most important are humility (7%) and purpose (5%).

Among evangelical Christians, who are a subset of the larger group of self-identified Christians, the results are largely the same with one notable exception—more than eight out of ten (83%) evangelicals listed "passion for God" as an important trait for leaders, compared with 31% of all Christians. Passion for God was the number one trait evangelicals look for in a leader. Evangelicals selected integrity as the second most important leadership quality. But practically, where do those answers lead Christians? What are they really looking for in a leader they have to interact with on a daily basis? Put simply: what do Christian adults look for in a boss? The research also explored the kinds of characteristics people want to find in their boss.

Perhaps unsurprisingly, the same top two characteristics emerged when asking about important leadership qualities and important employer traits: integrity (57%) and authenticity (47%). But after that, the lists diverge. Whereas Christians value discipline, passion for God, and competence in their leaders, they want to actually work for a boss who is collaborative, competent, and humble. Passion for God drops from fourth place to seventh, perhaps reflecting people's recognition that the workplace is not necessarily filled with believers. Still, among evangelicals, finding a boss who is a believer remains the most important criterion in their job search. Younger Christians aged 18-39 are slightly more interested in collaboration and purpose than are Christians over 40. They are also much more likely than older adults to look for bosses who are humble, with nearly one-third (32%) of 18-39-year-olds listing humility as a key trait in a potential boss.

Who Is Leading in a Crisis of Leadership?

More than eight in ten (82%) Christians believe the United States is facing a crisis of leadership because there aren't enough leaders. So who are the people rising as leaders to meet that challenge?

More than half of Christians in this country identify themselves as leaders (58%). Yet, less than one-sixth (15%) say their primary leadership trait is integrity, the quality Christians were most likely to name as an important leadership trait. In fact, Christians are most likely to identify their primary leadership trait as competence (20%), followed by discipline (16%), collaboration (15%), integrity (15%), and authenticity (14%). Only 1% of Christians say they are best at being humble (it is perhaps ironic that anyone would self-describe in this manner). Evangelicals are cut from a different bolt of cloth, naming passion for God as their best leadership quality (42%), compared with only 4% who named competence as their defining leadership trait.

Leaders were also asked what they would most like to improve about their leadership, using the same list of ten traits. The area where they said they want the most help is courage (27%), followed by a desire to grow in terms of discipline (17%), vision (15%), and passion for God (13%). Evangelical leaders are most similar to the broader Christian market in terms of their aspirations to improve as leaders: they want to grow in courage (27%), discipline (25%), passion for God (14%), and vision (9%).

Your Calling or Just a Job?

Many people discuss a job or career in terms of "calling." It's prevalent in much of the writings and conversations surrounding the topic of leadership. Particularly among Christians, one's occupation is often talked about in relation to God's "calling." And yet, only about one-third of Christians (34%) feel called to the work they currently do (among those who are presently employed). This is much higher among evangelicals (55%) but still reflects a huge gap in terms of the Christian community's sense of divine purpose in their work. Others say they "do not feel called" (19%), indicate they are "not sure" (13%), or admit they have "never thought about it before" (34%).

Younger Christians are less likely to feel called to their work than do older Christians (31% versus 36%). However, older Christians are even more likely than the younger Christians to confess they have never really considered the idea of being called to their current role (26% versus 38%).

So, if many Christians don't necessarily feel called to the work they're doing, what does that mean? The Barna study asked employed Christian adults if they believe God is calling them to do something else in terms of work, but they have not been willing to make a change yet because of their current life situation. Overall, about one out of ten working Christians (9%) agreed strongly with that feeling and another quarter (26%) agreed somewhat, totaling one-third of today's employed Christians (35%) who are experiencing this kind of tension about their calling. Among younger Christians, though, nearly half (44%) are feeling this disconnect between their perceived calling from God and the realities of their current employment.

When asked if they believe a person's calling lasts a lifetime, on balance, most people disagree rather than agree (68% versus 32%). In fact, only 4% strongly agree that a person can see what he or she is called to do from an early age.

What It All Means

1. Christians perceive a significant leadership crisis in America

caused by a distinct lack of leaders. Most feel they are leaders, but many of them aren't confident that their leadership abilities are the most important traits in a leader. This suggests many of them are still striving to meet even their own leadership expectations, and it also means many Christians may not think of their own leadership as helping to fill the leadership gap they experience. Perhaps this is why they are most interested in growing in terms of courage.

2. Evangelicals are far more likely than all self-described Christians to say passion for God is an essential leadership quality. That suggests evangelicals are much more comfortable working for people who share their beliefs and may not believe non-Christian bosses they work for are great leaders. In an increasingly secular context, evangelicals will have to navigate working with and for leaders who have a different definition of effective leadership.

3. It's illuminating to learn how few Christians believe they're called to do what they do. This data presents a challenge to the popular Christian understanding of career as calling since most Christians in the U.S. don't seem to be thinking about their jobs in terms of calling. Most of the data suggest the concept of calling is not on their radar. If people don't feel as if they're being called to their job, does that really matter to the quality of the work they do or the lives they maintain? It is worth noting the trend that younger Christians feel more of a desire to see their career as a calling and are more discontent when they feel a disconnect between their career and calling. However, is this perceived disconnect simply the reality of finding a fulfilling job when you're young and inexperienced especially in a bad economy? Is it the common angst of young people trying to figure out the purpose of their life? Or is it a sign of a growing trend among Christians to connect their faith more holistically with their life, a desire not to

compartmentalize faith, life, and work? Additional research and study is needed to clarify the connection between calling, leadership, and faith.

(**Note:** Research Releases in Culture & Media • June 3, 2013)

A compassionate leader seeks to understand and value the thoughts of his or her followers. To this end, open the dialogue and discussion with "what's on your mind" and seek ways to work toward a conclusion or stated the desired outcome. One of the many ways to achieve this is to analyze the Positive Performance Checklist below. When your staff feels included in the day-to-day affairs of the organization, productivity increases and performance improves as a result of the relationships that are formed.

Positive Performance Checklist

During a speech in July 2018 titled, "Lead with an Infinite Mind," Simon Sinek questioned the title: CEO. He asked us in the audience, "What do they do?" "Instead, we should rename the CEO, the CVO—Chief Vision Officer." Sinek states that we should reward the behavior, not the performance. Middle managers can practice leading so that when they arrive to senior leadership, they are who they want to be to lead.

While I agree in principle with Sinek, my experiences have revealed that behavior is the driver toward better performance. As leaders, we are empowered to create a workplace where people can and will thrive, excel, and surpass their own self-absorbed goals. One of the many ways to accomplish this goal is by affirming an environment that empowers others to tap into their creative minds that will produce results beyond what can be imagined.

There are several ways to complete the Positive Performance Checklist below. You want to simply complete this checklist and make changes in how you approach your workspace and time. You could also use it as a conversation starter. Have your team or department head peers complete the checklist and then meet to review how colleagues feel about the work environment.

✓ We spend time appreciating past successes and savoring the feeling of earlier accomplishments.

✓ We spend time envisioning how our work will make a difference in the future.

✓ We declare and commit to specific goals.

✓ We teach, encourage, and practice mindfulness in the workplace.

✓ We work in a culture that respects the need for recovery.

✓ We model positive performance behaviors by turning off email, cell phones, and texts during personal time and encouraging employees to use their vacation time.

✓ We teach and use active, constructive responding.

✓ We intentionally use language to prime others for success.

✓ We begin meetings with good news—either personal or work-related.

✓ We regularly celebrate the successes of our teams.

✓ We verbalize our appreciation and gratitude for co-workers on a routine basis.

✓ We use positive, upbeat language even when dealing with setbacks.

✓ We always include "because" when we ask for change.

✓ We interrogate our goals by asking, "Given our current reality and our future commitments, will we really reach our desired outcome?"

✓ We focus on and celebrate the process of working for a goal, rather than the outcome.

 ✓ We practice communicating positive expectations that bring out the best in our co-workers.

 ✓ We have a manager/employee feedback ratio of at least three positive comments to every negative one.

 ✓ We foster an environment that encourages lifetime learning and development.

(**Source:** Association for Talent Development, www.td.org/ATDtools)

Final Thoughts

Leadership is communication. That may sound too simple to be true, but it's a fact that good leaders and bad leaders are distinguished by how they communicate. Analyze the type of problems that commonly arise and you'll discover that most of these problems find their roots in poor communication.

"The tongue of the wise adorns knowledge, but the mouth of the fool gushes folly."

—Proverbs 15:2 (NIV)

Upon examination of the heart of the leader (as the messenger), we tap into the emotion, will, and intellect. People first buy into the leader, then their vision. Thus, every message that people receive is filtered through the messenger (as the leader) who delivers it. This requires compassion. Dr. Martin Luther King, Jr., Mrs. Flowers, and Deacon Ross are able to clearly communicate with me because each of them enabled me to buy into their leadership style. Understanding and trust precede action. Will you make the necessary adjustments in how you lead others?

STUDY QUESTIONS
& DISCUSSION

1. Do you believe that it's possible to get buy-in to your vision without forming meaningful relationships first? Why or why not?

_____

_____

_____

_____

_____

2. Do you lead with compassion? How?

_____

_____

_____

_____

_____

3. Describe Proverbs 15:2 in your own words.

_____

_____

_____

_____

4. Are you conscious of your communication style and how it may accentuate OR dilute your message?

_____

_____

_____

_____

_____

5. How well do you connect with your team /audience?

_____

_____

_____

_____

_____

PART THREE:

the RESULT of Servant Leadership: *Leading Others*

"Peace I leave with you; my peace I give you. I do not give to you as the world gives. Do not let your hearts be troubled and do not be afraid."
—John 14:27 (New International Version)

CHAPTER SEVEN

Leading with Passion

"Take pains with these things; be absorbed in them, so that your progress may be evident to all."

—1 Timothy 4:15 (New American Standard Bible)

"You're blessed when you get your inside world—your mind and heart—put right. Then you can see God in the outside world."

—Matthew 5:8 (The Message)

On September 28, 2018, as one of three keynote speakers, I stood before an audience of 150 professionals whose charge is to advocate for at-risk youth and their families. These professionals also work daily alongside people with disabilities to offer them opportunities to contribute to our society in a positive and productive way. The organization they represent, Nexus Youth and Family Solutions, hired me to teach one of my favorite topics, *"Becoming a Person of Influence,"* to their group of leaders from across the U.S.A. at their 7th annual national training conference in Plymouth, Minnesota. This day was so special to me because Nexus' mission and vision align with my life story over the past fifty-plus years.

I am the sibling of a mentally disabled brother and the father of an autistic son. My brother, Eric, was born in 1964 on the U.S. Marine Corps base at Camp LeJeune, North Carolina. During a routine check-up, it was discovered that his brain did not receive sufficient oxygen while in the womb, thus, retarding his normal development. It was documented that he had a mental deficiency that would last a lifetime. As a result, my childhood, youth, and young adulthood years were spent helping my parents care for my brother. Advocating with school teachers and administration, protection from bullies, driving to scheduled appointments and selecting which clothes to wear were just some of my responsibilities in support of my younger brother. Many years later after I began a family with my wife Gail, our third child Cameron was born in 1998 in Princeton, New Jersey. The physicians on duty documented this as a normal birth, seemingly no complications. However, we noticed that Cameron did not speak a word during his initial two years. When we had him examined in 2000 during a routine check-up, it was discovered that he was autistic. This was the cause of his non-communication. Similar to my responsibilities in caring for my brother Eric, I would now repeat these identical practices for my son Cameron to ensure his readiness for a world that may not treat him with respect and dignity because of his disability.

For a full hour, I shared my life circumstances in a very personal way advocating for Eric and Cameron during my keynote speech at Nexus's national training conference. Through my passion on the topic, combined with several personal antidotes on how I overcame the myriad of challenges, I touched the hearts of the leaders in the audience as expressed through their kind words at the conclusion of my session. The CEO, Dr. Michelle Murray, immediately extended an invitation to me to join the board of directors. I was so touched and humbled by the invitation that I said "Yes" without hesitation. On that day, I learned two valuable lessons about leading with passion:

1) Passion ➔ Compassion ➔ Action. Leaders who are passionate about a topic, person, activity, or event are compelled to show compassion toward the cause which determines the action we take to improve the situation or circumstance.

2) The action we take, with the proper amount of passion, zeal, inspiration, and motivation will move our audience in a manner where, perhaps, an invitation to join their team is a show of how they value our contribution.

Do Workers Want Feedback or Not?

Management guru Marcus Buckingham has a bone to pick with one of the prevailing trends in management wisdom: that companies need to get better at giving tough, candid feedback and need to do it more often. As indicative of the trend, he points to such recent popular books as Bridgewater Associates chief executive Ray Dalio's *Principles* and Kim Scott's *Radical Candor*, the proliferation of employee survey tools and feedback apps like 15Five and news reports about tough internal cultures like the ones at Amazon or Netflix.

> Marcus Buckingham of ADP Research Institute says that the standard "theory of excellence is wrong...Excellence is not homogeneous" and cannot be reduced to a list of attributes of competencies.

In a news article in the Harvard Business Review called "The Feedback Fallacy," Buckingham and his co-author, Cisco executive Ashley Goodall, argue that managers are getting it all wrong. Managers who focus so much on candid feedback are ignoring research that shows how hard it is for people to rate the performances of others and that shows how difficult it is to standardize and homogenize what "excellence" looks like in different people.

"The big fear of companies is misalignment and lack of control, which is understandable," Buckingham says. "The problem, of course, is that the value of a human being is the uniqueness of a human being. That's the value. That's the feature. Not something to be solved. Or try to fix."

Managers obviously do have to coach their employees toward better performance and let their people know, somehow, when they've messed up. So how should they talk to employees? We spoke with Buckingham about what he thinks most companies get wrong, what millennials really want when it comes to feedback (his teenage daughter is an Instagram influencer), and what managers should look for. (Clue: It's not whether workers fit neatly into all seven "competencies" or "attributes" in the typical performance review.) Here are a couple of key questions/statements for the leader's consideration:

Q: You've written about why companies should focus on employee strengths, not weaknesses, and the problems with traditional performance reviews. What's new here?

A: *What you see now is a horde of people running down a path at great speed, combined with technology, trying to create a world in which, number one, everybody is more continuously giving feedback because we think the problem is we don't give enough. Number two, we think millennials in the workplace crave feedback. I'll do 50 speeches a year, and every single company has made a god of feedback.*

Q: You say it's wrong to think millennials want more feedback at work.

A: *What a misdiagnosis that is. They love attention. That's totally different. For instance, Instagram is about building an audience. What*

you're looking for is each little heart is a positive affirmation of an
audience. They're not looking for constructive, candid, or radically
candid feedback. My daughter has 14 million Instagram followers, and
what Lilla wants is an audience. She's not looking for feedback. She's
looking for interaction.

(**Note 1:** *The Washington Post*, Business Section, February 24, 2019, by Jena McGregor)

What Every Leader Needs to Know About Followers

A New Typology

The typology that Barbara Kellerman, a James MacGregor Burns Lecturer in Public Leadership at the Center for Public Leadership at Harvard University's John F. Kennedy School of Government, developed after years of study and observation aligns followers on one, all-important metric level of engagement. She categorizes all followers according to where they fall along a continuum that ranges from "feeling and doing absolutely nothing" to "being passionately committed and deeply involved." She chose a level of engagement because regardless of context, it's the follower's degree of involvement that largely determines the nature of the superior-subordinate relationship. This is especially true today. Because of the aforementioned changes in the cultures and structures of organizations, for instance, knowledge workers often care as much if not more about intrinsic factors—the quality of their interpersonal relationships with their superiors, for instance, or their passion for the organization's mission—than about extrinsic rewards such as salary, titles, and other benefits.

A typology based on a single, simple metric as opposed to the multiple rating factors used by the creators of previous segmenting tools offers leaders immediate information on whether and to what degree their followers are buying what they're selling: Do your followers participate actively in meetings and proceedings? Do they demonstrate engagement by pursuing dialogues, asking good questions, and generating new ideas? Or have they checked out, pecking away at their Blackberries or keeping a close eye on the clock? She categorizes followers as *isolates*, *bystanders*, *participants*, *activists*, and *diehards*. Let's look at each type.

Isolates are completely detached. These followers are scarcely aware of what's going on around them. Moreover, they do not care about their leaders, know anything about them, or respond to them in any obvious way. Their alienation is, nevertheless, of consequence. By knowing and doing nothing, these types of followers passively support the status quo and further strengthen leaders who already have the upper hand. As a result, isolates can drag down their groups or organizations.

Isolates are most likely to be found in large companies where they can easily disappear in the maze of cubicles, offices, departments, and divisions. Their attitudes and behaviors attract little or no notice from those at the top levels of the organization as long as they do their jobs, even if only marginally well and with zero enthusiasm. Consider the member of the design team at a large consumer goods company who dutifully completes his individual assignments but couldn't care less about the rest of the company's products and processes; he just needs to pay the bills. Or witness the typical American voter, or more accurately, the nonvoter.

Bystanders observe but do not participate. These free-riders deliberately stand aside and disengage, both from their leaders and from their groups or organizations. They may go along passively when it is in their self-interest to do so, but they are not internally motivated to engage in an active way. Their withdrawal also amounts to tacit support for whoever and whatever constitutes the status quo.

Like isolates, bystanders can drag down the rest of the group or organization. But unlike isolates, they are perfectly aware of what is going on around them; they just choose not to take the time, the trouble, or to be fair, sometimes the risk to get involved. A notorious example from the public sector is people who refuse to intervene when a crime is being committed. This is commonly referred to as the Genovese syndrome or the bystander effect. A corporate counterpart might be the account representative at a financial services company who goes along with the new CEO's recently mandated process changes, even as some of her colleagues are being demoted or fired for pointing out inefficiencies in the new system. To speak up or get involved would be to put her own career and reputation on the line at a time when the CEO is still weeding out "loyal" employees from "problem" ones.

Participants are engaged in some way. Whether these followers clearly support their leaders and organizations or clearly oppose them, they care enough to invest some of what they have (time or money, for example) to try to make an impact. Consider the physicians and scientists who developed the painkiller Vioxx. They felt personally invested in producing a best-selling drug for Merck, bringing it to market, and defending it even in the face of later revelations that the drug could create very serious side effects in some users. They were driven by their own passions (ambition, innovation, creation, helping people)—not necessarily by senior managers.

Activists feel strongly one way or another about their leaders and organizations, and they act accordingly. These followers are eager, energetic, and engaged. They are heavily invested in people and processes, so they work hard either on behalf of their leaders or to undermine and even unseat them.

Activists who strongly support their leaders and managers can be important allies, whether they are direct or indirect reports. Activists are not necessarily high in number because oftentimes their level of commitment demands an expense of time and energy that most people find difficult to sustain. Of course, this same passion also means they can and often do have a considerable impact on a group or organization. Those activists who are as loyal as they are competent and committed are frequently in the leader or manager's inner circle simply because they can be counted on to dedicate their (usually long) working hours to the mission as their superiors see it.

Diehards are prepared to go down for their cause whether it's an individual, an idea, or both. These followers may be deeply devoted to their leaders, or they may be strongly motivated to oust their leaders by any means necessary. They exhibit an all-consuming dedication to someone or something they deem worthy.

Of course, not all diehard followers are so extreme in their devotion. But they are willing, by definition, to endanger their own health and welfare in the service of their cause. Soldiers the world over, for instance, risk life and limb in their commitment to protect and defend. They are trained and willing to follow nearly blindly the orders of their superiors who depend absolutely on them to get the job done.

As mentioned earlier, attitudes and opinions do not matter much when we are talking about isolates and bystanders, if only because they do little or even nothing. They matter a great deal, however, when we are talking about participants, activists, and diehards. Do these followers support their leader? Or, rank notwithstanding, are they using their available resources to resist people in positions of power, authority, and influence? This typology suggests that good leaders should pay special attention to those who demonstrate their strong support or their vehement opposition. It's not difficult to see the signs: participants and especially activists and diehards wear their hearts on their sleeves.

(**Note 2:** *Harvard Business Review*, by Barbara Kellerman, December 2007, hbr.org)

Manager versus Leader

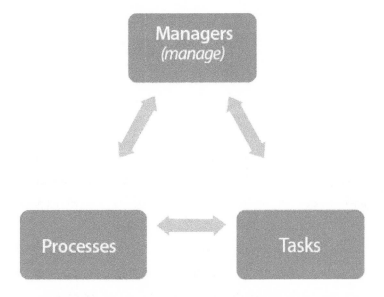

The diagrams below will help us to understand the key differences between a manager and a leader. Simply put, managers 'manage' processes, actions, and tasks, whereas, leaders 'lead' people.

Managers are responsible for the efficient and effective day-to-day operation of an organization's processes, practices, tasks, and or actions. In doing so, great managers ensure that the company, government, academia, non-profit, and church run smoothly and is aligned with the stated mission, vision, strategic priorities, and guiding principles. Good processes, automated systems, and smooth coordination of daily actions add to a workplace that is conducive to excellence.

The Leader
(leads)

Senior-
level

Mid-
level

Front-
line

Leaders, on the other hand, are charged to lead the people. Leaders take care of the team that was hired to handle the work. A good leader creates an environment that fosters high performers and increases productivity through relationship building, trust, integrity, and character. Leaders do not micro-manage the staff, but instead, seek ways to support the staff. In doing so, the front-line, mid-level, and senior-level staff feels encouraged and comfortable to make valuable contributions to both the team and organization.

Final Thoughts

In his article, "How to Overcome Resistance," columnist Scott Mann, a former Green Beret and founder of Rooftop Leadership, reminds us that *"As leaders, we face a multitude of enemies—the erosion of trust, distraction, disengagement from purpose, and anything that will put itself between you and the tracks you want to leave and the impact you want to make. But I believe resistance is the greatest enemy you will ever face in your quest to achieve something bigger than yourself."* When he was thirty-eight years old, in a sermon given shortly before he died, Reverend Dr. Martin Luther King, Jr. whose 90th birthday would have been January 15, 2019, talked about living until age ninety: *"You may be thirty-eight years old, as I happen to be, and one day some great opportunity stands before you and calls upon you to stand up for some great principle, some great issue, some great cause. You refuse to do it because you are afraid... Well, you may go on and live until you are ninety, but you are just as dead at thirty-eight as you would be at ninety."*

(**Note 3**: *AARP* Magazine, January/February 2019, page 4.)

Desire is that insatiable urge, longing, appetite, craving, and yearning to stretch for something greater than you are right now. *"Delight thyself also in the LORD: and he shall give thee the desires of thine heart"* (Psalm 37:4, KJV). Passion pulls us up enabling us to overcome adversity. Passion pulls us out giving us initiative. Passion positions us well giving us the greatest odds for success.

STUDY QUESTIONS & DISCUSSION

1. How well do you motivate your team? Explain.

_____

_____

_____

_____

_____

2. Are your zeal and enthusiasm evident to your team? How do you know?

_____

_____

_____

_____

_____

3. Does the organization you lead measure its performance?

_____

_____

_____

_____

4. In your opinion, does your style of influence match what is written in 1 Timothy 4:15?

_____

_____

_____

_____

_____

5. Passion is contagious. Does your team match the passion that you demonstrate?

_____

_____

_____

_____

_____

CHAPTER EIGHT

Leading to Equip

"If anything is needed today, it is leaders who are willing to take a stand and who are willing to do what is right, regardless of whether or not it is politically correct. Leaders who are strong and courageous are very scarce, both in the world and in the Church."

—Rick Renner
Author, *Insights on Successful Leadership*

"The wise in heart will receive commandments: but a prating fool shall fall."

—Proverbs 10:8 (Kings James Version)

F atherhood is the joy of my life! I believe that leadership begins in the home and that's where I learned to lead my family through the good times and the many, many challenges this life presents. The skills, principles, and practices that I learned at home transitioned with relative ease into the workplace at the entry-level and then continued as a mid-level and senior-level leader during my 34-year career. My wife, Gail, was also a benefactor of meaningful and strategic leadership acumen as we raised our children together in love and with compassion.

Equipping the next generation of leaders, for me, began over twenty years with the arrival of my first son, Kevin, in 1995. He came into our lives through the Bethany Christian Services adoption agency in Crofton, Maryland. My good friend Minister Paulette Holloway was the new director at the time, and Kevin was the first infant from that agency who she placed with a lovely and willing family—Gail and me. As the proud dad of this baby boy, we elected to give him my first name which means "*kind*." Kevin's story is very unique and quickly prepared me for leadership given his condition at birth. He was born in December 1995 as a premature baby in a Baltimore, Maryland, hospital at two pounds, four ounces. His young parents, after receiving the appropriate and timely counseling, elected to place him with an adoption agency in hopes that a lovely family would come along to equip him with love, a good home environment, and a bright future. After a few interviews with the team at Bethany, all involved agreed that we could meet little Kevin (not his name at the time) and hold him for the first time. This meeting took place in early March 1996 on a sunny Saturday afternoon at the Crofton, Maryland, office. Given his size and barely three months old, little Kevin was dressed in a blue and red plaid outfit, had a head full of hair and a four-ounce bottle of milk in both hands as his foster mother released him into my arms. Within a few seconds, he smiled and said, "Da." That single moment sealed the deal. We agreed to proceed with the adoption process and officially bring little Kevin into our lives as our first son.

Fast forward eleven months later from little Kevin's birthday, my second son was born in a Silver Spring, Maryland, hospital in November 1996. This was Gail's first natural birth and she remained in labor for over twelve hours. We were in a local grocery store on a

Saturday afternoon near our home when the labor pains began. She let out a groan as we walked the aisles of the store and said, "I think it's time." I responded by hastily escorting her to my car. With overnight bags already packed and in the car, we left the grocery store and traveled directly to the hospital where the team of doctors, nurses, anesthesiologists, and assistants greeted us upon our arrival. I assisted Gail as much as I could in the delivery room. Breathing techniques that we learned in class and strategies to keep her calm were overshadowed by the pain she was experiencing. Watching the tubes, needles, and other medications going in and on her body caused me to get nauseous to the point where I fainted for a brief period. We remained in the hospital overnight until the doctor finally reported that the baby was getting closer to arrival the next Sunday morning. As I took my position by Gail's side to cut the baby's umbilical cord, I was quickly pushed to the side by the medical team because it was wrapped around the neck causing a loss of needed oxygen. We named our second son Christopher. Beyond that one issue in the delivery room, Gail had a normal birth, and Christopher was a bundle of joy to us as we watched him grow to achieve many wonderful milestones.

Fifteen months later, our third son was born at the Princeton University Hospital in Princeton, New Jersey, in early April 1998. Gail carried him for a full term with no complications or difficulties. By now, we were in full swing of raising baby boys and thoroughly enjoying the experience and new life as young parents. We named our third son Cameron. He was a very quiet baby who did not say anything, rarely cried nor did he make any vocal gestures. During his first year, we did not question this much. However, as this continued into his second year, we grew concerned. This was unusual. After Cameron celebrated his 2nd birthday, we took him to the Newark Autism Center in Newark,

New Jersey, for an examination and possible diagnosis. As Gail suspected, Cameron was diagnosed with autism.

Autism is a serious developmental disorder that impairs the ability to communicate and interact. Autism spectrum disorder impacts the nervous system. Treatment can help, but this condition can't be cured. As we studied and learned about this ailment that would impact his life as well as his overall lifestyle, I took the lead to ensure that our state and county would provide the requisite support for him to ensure that he would have access to the best services available. Interestingly, I had had *some* experience with assisting my younger brother, Eric, who was born with a mental disability in 1964. Few resources were available at that time to support Eric. I helped my mom and dad as best I could, but with Cameron, it was much different because he was my child and caring for him was my responsibility. Fortunately for Cameron, living in Somerset County, New Jersey, and then Howard County, Maryland, we always had access to the best teachers, schools, school administrators, community assistance, government programs, and private caretakers. But it required much research, effort, and persistence to understand what was available through these local resources and tenacity to study and learn about the plethora of information that is available. This taught me that leaders are readers!

In each instance with our three sons, the condition of their births prepared me with the necessary leadership skills that would be required to equip them for alignment with their purpose and God's plan for their lives. As they progressed through pre-school, elementary, middle, high school, and college despite some learning challenges, I made the necessary adjustments and modifications to lead and equip them for their next step as boys and young men. Again, leadership begins at home. This was my humble beginning and introduction to becoming a leader.

Leadership Development

On February 8, 2018, Ashley Ansari of InnovaSystems International LLC published a well-read blog titled "7 Statistics You Can't Ignore About Leadership Development." The blog reads in part:

Leadership. It's the skill that finds its way into just about every cover letter, job description, and career page. Candidates pursue careers that support leadership development while talent acquisition teams dream of applicants with leadership skills. Unfortunately, this often creates a chicken or the egg situation where organizations aren't prepared to train for the leadership roles they expect employees to take. Unfortunately, employees never make it into higher-level roles they could excel at, or they end up earning management positions they aren't qualified to hold. Leaders aren't born, they're made, right? Unfortunately, these leadership development statistics unveil a bit of dissonance in how companies are leading their leaders:

- 77% of organizations report they're currently experiencing a leadership gap.

- U.S. companies spent $160 billion on employee training and education.

- 83% of organizations say it is important to develop leaders at all levels.

- Only 10% of CEOs believe their company's leadership development initiatives have a clear business impact.

- 89% of executives surveyed believe strengthening organizational leadership is a top priority.

- 63% of millennials said their leadership skills were not being fully developed.

- 81% of employees reporting to recently trained managers said they were more engaged in their job.

Oprah Winfrey reminds us to "Be Your Truest Self in Service of Others." During her keynote address before 13,500 attendees from fifty-five countries, she challenged an audience of talent development professionals, with an emphasis on the conference theme "Focus on Leadership." Winfrey stated, "Follow your gut, get good leaders, and be of service. . . . What I understand and know for sure, is that we share a common language: truth. We all want to live out the truest expression of ourselves as human beings." She noted that things have only gone wrong in her life when she didn't listen to her gut and when she chose the wrong leadership. "Good leadership is everything," she said. She noted that we are all here to offer our gifts and talents and to use them in service to something or someone other than ourselves. Indeed, each day is a beautiful day.

(**Note 1**: 2019 Association for Talent Development International Conference, Washington, DC, Opening Keynote, May 20, 2019, by the ATD staff.)

Mentoring Minds Want to Know

Many people attribute part of their professional success to having a mentor. To learn more about this, Olivet Nazarene University surveyed 3,000 people about professional mentor-mentee relationships to see what they look like in 2019. Here's what the survey found:

- 76% of people think mentors are important, but only 37% of people currently have one.
- Most people opt for same-sex mentors (69% women; 82% men).
- People with mentors are happier at their current jobs than those without.
- Only 14% of mentor relationships started by asking someone to be their mentor; 61% of those relationships developed naturally.
- The average length of current mentorships is 3.3 years.

- The frequency of in-person meetings is less than once per month (excluding instances where mentors/mentees interact daily).
- The average time spent talking per month is 4 hours.

(**Note 2:** *Training* magazine, May/June 2019, page 7, www.online.olivet.edu/research-statistics-on-professional-mentors)

What is Mentoring?

Mentoring is someone sharing his or her wisdom, expertise, insight, and perspectives to enhance personal and professional growth in another individual. Connecting with a mentor is one of the most effective things you can do to enhance your career.

It is defined as a long-term relationship focused on supporting the growth and development of the mentee. Usually, the mentor is older (not always) and has more experience in a particular area than does the mentee. The mentor's assistance helps the mentee enhance his or her professional and or personal growth. Mentors typically share knowledge, skills, and advice to assist the mentee in his or her career growth.

A **Mentor** is a "*guide/expert.*"

While **coaching** and **mentoring** offer some of the same expertise, coaching is a more collaborative effort which focuses on improving specific goals or tasks, while mentoring is a long term relationship which can provide guidance throughout a person's career.

What is Coaching?

Coaching is a confidential, customized, high-touch, developmental activity that involves partnering with a specially trained professional who assists individuals or teams in achieving their personal and or professional goals and improving their organizational impact. Coaches honor individuals as experts in their lives and organizations.

They support individuals in delivering their creativity and resourcefulness so they may become their best whole selves.

It is defined as a helping relationship formed between a client who has managerial authority and responsibility in an organization and a consultant who uses a wide variety of behavioral techniques and methods to assist the client achieve a mutually identified set of goals to improve his or her professional performance and personal satisfaction and consequently to improve the effectiveness of the client's organization within a formally defined coaching agreement.

A **Coach** is a "*thinking partner.*"

Prior to the start of all mentoring and coaching sessions, I suggest that the participants respond in writing to these five important questions. The preparation form that is presented to the participants should be the focus of the subsequent sessions toward the desired outcome:

1. What is the subject I want to discuss?
2. What do I want to achieve from this session?
3. What action did I take since my last session with my last coach?
4. What do I want to be held accountable for?
5. What else would make this session the most productive and move me in the direction of my goals/objectives?

Coaching vs. Mentoring – What's the Difference?

	Coach	Mentor
Purpose	Growth/development, helping while also generating results	People realize their potential

Role	Learning/thinking partner	Learning/thinking partner; guide/expert
Process	Drawing out knowledge that resides within coachee; Questioning: coach engages in inquiry to guide the coachee	Sharing knowledge that resides within a mentor; Telling: Mentor shares expertise, offering answers, and solutions
Relationship	Generally, time-limited with a set duration	Ongoing relationship that can last for a long period of time
Focus	Helping coachee develop their own way of problem-solving	Helping mentee problem solve
Organizational Knowledge	May be somewhat limited, particularly if external coach	High level of knowledge about the organization
Skills Used	Listening, questioning, questioning, questioning	Listening, questioning, suggesting, advising, giving guidance

The Value Proposition of Coaching:

- Participants are able to receive customized, development activity under the guidance of a trained, certified coach.

- Helps to increase the pool of professionally-trained coaches and will help your organization to push coaching further down into the organization.

- Once participants have exposure to some basic coaching skills, they start using them with their teams and explore their successes and challenges in their peer coaching triads where they work with a coach to continue to develop their coaching skills.

- Following on from the initial session, participants are immediately aware that they are not buying some off-the-shelf personal development process. They're committing themselves to an ongoing and supportive relationship.

Types of Assessments:

- Personality Assessment: helps the participant to understand their unique personality type.
- 360-degree Assessment: helps the participant to accentuate their strengths and work to improve their weaknesses as a result of a self-assessment combined with assessments from peers, co-workers, direct reports, and bosses. The participants' blind spots will be revealed in a manner in which they can focus on self-reflection and self-development.
- Emotional Intelligence Assessment: helps the participant to learn self-control strategies and techniques that foster their ability to remain under control in all situations.
- Conflict Style Assessment: helps by participating in navigating the undeniable face-to-face conflict that will happen in the workplace.

The diagram below illustrates the unique nature of the coaching alliance and demonstrates where the power flows. Notice how the participant grants power to the relationship and is empowered by it and how the coach also grants power to the relationship, and yet all the power returns to the participant, not the coach.

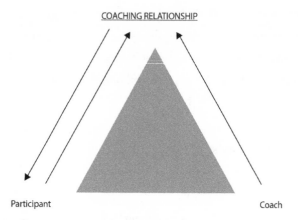

COACHING RELATIONSHIP

Participant   Coach

The Learning Cycle

Leaders must become familiar with 'The Learning Cycle.' The four stages of learning apply to every person and can help us understand their current state of mind. They are as follows:

Stage 1: Unconscious Incompetence

- Very little *performance* goes on at this stage, and there's no understanding as to why.

- When unconsciously incompetent, you simply aren't aware that you're not able to do something. For example, a young child isn't consciously aware that he or she can't drive because he or she has not even considered the process of driving.

Stage 2: Conscious Incompetence

- At the next stage, conscious incompetence, a person *becomes aware of their existing inability*, recognizing flaws and weak areas. For example, the child becomes a teenager and becomes aware that he or she can't drive like slightly older teenagers or their parents.

Stage 3: Conscious Competence

- This is where *performance improves* and effort is more conscious and somewhat contrived. The teenager has passed his or her driving test but still has to think about how he or she goes about driving.

Stage 4: Unconscious Competence

• Finally, the person arrives at being unconsciously competent, where *natural, integrated, higher levels of performance are achieved* entirely unconsciously. Think of how that teenager has grown up to be you, and now think about your driving experience. I bet you rarely think about how you drive if at all!

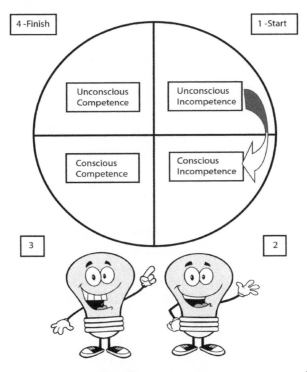

> If your church, ministry or organization doesn't have to deal with the challenges of growth, it is a signal that something is obviously unhealthy in the organization.

> God is not obliged to use everyone who prays, "God, please use me!" Neither are you obligated to use everyone who shows up and says he or she feels called to be a part of your team. For many are called, but few are chosen. (Matthew 22:14, King James Version)

Equipping people is a unique skill that helps them to stay on track with their goals in a manner that suits them. As it pertains to personal growth, people tend to stay motivated based upon their personality type. I have been taught by my senior mentor John C. Maxwell that "motivation gets you going, but discipline keeps you growing." If you choose a system that suits you, then you will have a better chance at succeeding. It's referred to as the Law of Consistency in John's book titled, *The 15 Invaluable Laws of Growth*. Below are four personality types to consider and how each type focuses on one's growth and development (equipping):

PERSONALITY TYPE	CHARACTERISTICS
Phlegmatic	• **Strength**: easy-going, likable • **Weakness**: inertia • **Focus toward growth**: Find value in what you need to do that you've yet to start. Become tenacious for the goals on the horizon.
Choleric	• **Strength**: take charge, decision-makers • **Weakness**: if they aren't "in charge," they refuse to participate; need control • **Focus toward growth**: Tap your internal motivation by focusing on the choices you can make and take charge.
Sanguine	• **Strength**: life of the party, fun-loving • **Weakness**: lack of focus • **Focus toward growth**: Make it a game. Reward yourself along the way as you level-up your growth and make incremental progress.

Melancholic	• **Strength:** attention to detail and excellence in their work • **Weakness:** fear of making mistakes • **Focus toward growth:** Focus your energy on the joy in learning over the fear of failing. Your goal is to become a master of a subject; go after it fearlessly.

State of the Industry (*on trust . . . transparency . . . connection*)

Humanity prepared whitepaper for the human resources community to examine the current state of the human capital management market. It evaluates the challenges in employee scheduling, schedule forecasting, time clock, *training*, and leave/vacation management not only for human resource professionals but also for line managers and supervisors, as well as employees themselves.

Modern organizations of all sizes and in a wide variety of vertical markets recognize that long-term success is dependent on trust, transparency, and connection, not only with their customers but also in how management and employees connect and interact.

"Organizations of all sizes have an ongoing need to monitor, manage, and optimize tactical, day-to-day workforce functions so departments and teams function effectively."

Managing employees and talent has never been more challenging than it is today. Businesses now exist in an era where real-time is the de facto standard, information is expected to be a single mouse-click or finger-tap away, and both skilled and unskilled talent can be challenging to find and retain. Human Resource departments and line managers need accurate, up-to-the-minute information to make solid, strategic decisions that result in business success. Employee scheduling, training, and on-boarding progress, payroll, revenue/business forecasting, vacation and employee availability status, and workforce budgeting and reporting are key business factors that not only require real-time analytics but a collaborative effort across the entire organization—HR management and the employees themselves. Compounding these issues is the critical need for employee access to real-time information and engagement both with management and with each other for tactical issues that face businesses every day: scheduling and shift changes, payroll issues, on-boarding, and ongoing training.

Effective employee management used to simply mean having the right employees in the right positions. And for businesses, it also meant having adequate staffing dependent on seasonality and sales trends. Business managers and HR professionals are keenly aware that employees who are well trained and managed effectively and efficiently are better prepared to do their jobs and serve patrons and clients, thus leading to happy customers, deeper employee satisfaction, rising profits, and a measurable increase in repeat business.

Contrarily, untrained employees who are mismanaged or untrained can wreak havoc on a business chipping away not only at corporate success, but also corporate culture and employee morale. Employees unfamiliar with products, services, or corporate processes can't effectively engage customers, creating animosity and resentment. And mis-scheduled staff can not only create frustrated customers who might choose to take their business and money elsewhere but also unhappy employees who feel unsuccessful and resentful towards the organization and their manager. Too often these issues result in sustained drops in business, lower revenue, high employee turnover, and in today's social media-centric world, warding off potential customers and top talent through negative online reviews on websites like Yelp and Glassdoor.

(**Note 3:** Humanity [whitepaper] – Powerful, Intuitive Employee Scheduling ©2018)

Final Thoughts

Leaders are readers. Reading one hour per day in your chosen field will make you an international expert in seven years. This is why I recommend to all my students to read one book each month! Here are some surprising book facts:

For leaders to equip those who follow, it is imperative to lead them by our example. Read!

(**Note 4:** ©RobertBrewer.org / The Jenkins Group, Brian Tracy)

STUDY QUESTIONS & DISCUSSION

1. How well does your team work together? Give at least two examples.

_____

_____

_____

_____

_____

2. Identify two ways that you equip your team for leadership responsibilities.

_____

_____

_____

_____

_____

3. What comes first: (1) Assigning a task to someone on your team based upon the potential that you see in them, OR (2) Assigning a task to the person on your team who has demonstrated that they can accomplish a desired task? Why?

_____

_____

_____

_____

_____

4. Are you more successful in reproducing a leader who is introverted or extroverted? Explain your answer.

_____

_____

_____

_____

_____

5. Are you cultivating the potential of those on your team as a means to developing leaders?

_____

_____

_____

_____

_____

CHAPTER NINE

Passing the Baton

"And Moses was an hundred and twenty years old when he died: his eye was not dim, nor his natural force abated. And the children of Israel wept for Moses in the plains of Moab thirty days: so the days of weeping and mourning for Moses were ended. And Joshua the son of Nun was full of the spirit of wisdom; for Moses had laid his hands upon him: and the children of Israel hearkened unto him, and did as the LORD commanded Moses."

—Deuteronomy 34:7-9 (King James Version)

"Day after day they met in the temple [area] continuing with one mind, and breaking bread in various private homes. They were eating their meals together with joy and generous hearts."

—Acts 2:46 (Amplified)

For over twenty years in the workplace, it was standard practice for me to pass the baton to the next leaders as I elected to move on to my next leadership assignment. It was deliberate and purposeful. My preference was to always, to the maximum extent possible, hire the next leader from within. Leaders have a responsibility to teach, coach, mentor, and train the person coming behind us for the purpose of transition and consistency.

As a mid-to-senior-level leader in a key leadership position in New York, New York, I hired a deputy to serve under me in a large government regional office. The year was 1996. This was my first management job following my graduation upon completion of the Executive Potential Program. I was selected by the senior leaders to transition from headquarters in Washington, DC, to the field office in New York, leading a medium-sized team into the future after a massive agency-wide reorganization. I knew that I would be in my position for about thirty-six months and needed to ensure that a dedicated professional would buy into the mission, vision, and structure that I would create in this new organization and carry it to higher heights. The person I selected for the deputy position interviewed very well and, once hired, was a perfect fit for the job at hand. We worked closely together during my tenure. He was a quick learner, and he executed successfully on the strategic priorities that I communicated to the team, including staff and stakeholders throughout the region. At the conclusion of my appointment in 1999, I recommended that the deputy resume my responsibilities as head of the organization. My recommendation was accepted.

> *Nothing is more important in your organization than the people you choose for its leadership.*

My final position before retirement in October 2017, was Chief of Staff of one of our joint military–government–contractor organizations within the Department of Defense. In this role, I was responsible for overseeing and leading many people and functions under my charge. Information technology has long been my weakness in terms of execution and implementation. Realizing this, during the interview phase as I searched for a Deputy Chief of Staff, it was imperative that the applicant have a strong background in information technology. It was one of the interview questions. After taking note of her strong resume and great interview skills, I hired our deputy with full confidence that she could be mentored to take over my responsibilities when I retired. As suspected, she was a phenomenal hire, exceeded expectations, demonstrated outstanding work ethic, and was subsequently recommended for my position. My recommendation was accepted.

Leaders must reproduce other leaders through our example, having a willingness to train, creating a growth environment, and ultimately, having discernment in hiring the right people.

A CEO's Perspective

Hamdi Ulukaya is the founder and CEO of Chobani, a business that produces Greek-style yogurt. In the spring of 2018, he addressed the graduating MBA class of the Wharton School business school at the University of Pennsylvania. Ulukaya, a Kurdish immigrant from Turkey, shared wisdom that points to integrity and character as essential aspects of business success. Some of the insightful lessons that he shared apply to all leaders who aspire to achieve remarkable results as he has done. His vision and execution is a model for all who will eventually pass the baton. Some of his lessons are mentioned below.

Resources Not the Crucial Issue

After arriving in New York City, Uhikaya moved upstate New York and started a cheese business. In 2005, an unprofitable Kraft yogurt factory in New Berlin, New York, came up for sale.

Where Kraft saw a shrinking business, Ulukaya saw entrepreneurial opportunities. Nobody was making quality yogurt for mass-market sale in supermarkets. He had few resources.

Many think money is the primary key to entrepreneurial success. Many see companies such as Chobani and Apple as rare exceptions, believing that start-up success is blocked to all but the wealthy or those who can raise money from venture capitalists.

Too much money and you may lose sight of what is essential which is solving an urgent need of consumers. Too much money and you may find, as the dot. com bust company Quokka did, that your budget for pricey Aeron chairs exceeds your annual revenue. Or, you may find yourself, as another well-capitalized bust Flooz did, spending 8 million dollars for celebrity spokesperson campaign by Whoopi Goldberg. Or, you may, as Chobani didn't, hire more employees than your current growth supports.

Too much money and you may lose sight of building your business culture on a foundation of purpose, principles, and values. Dee Hock, the founding CEO of Visa, observed this in his book, *One from Many: Visa and the Rise of Chaordic Organization*:

"An organization's success has enormously more to do with clarity of a shared purpose, common principles and strength of belief in them than to assets, expertise, operating ability, or management competence, important as they may be."

A Detailed Plan Is Not Crucial

Consistent with Hock's advice, Chobani had a strong sense of purpose from the beginning: the production of a higher quality mass-market yogurt. In five years, Chobani became the largest producer of Greek yogurt, with now over $1 billion in annual sales. To have such success, some assume Ulukaya must have had a bullet-proof, detailed business plan.

Initially, he re-hired four employees from the Kraft plant; these former employees thought Ulukaya had a "magic answer" to success. His first initiative was to paint the walls of the manufacturing facility. An employee said to Ulukaya, "Tell me you have more ideas than [painting the walls]."

Ulukaya recognized that organizational intelligence wasn't limited to his own; he and his team discovered each next step. Imbued principles, purpose, and values guided business decision-making without a complicated playbook. Charles Koch, CEO of Koch Industries, understands this well. In his book *The Science of Success*, Koch offers this advice:

"To function effectively, any group of people, whether a society or an organization, must be guided largely by general rules of just conduct, not just specific commands. Leaving the particulars to those doing the work encourages discovery. It also enhances adaptation to changing conditions."

Hock explained succinctly how to unleash the entrepreneurial discovery process in a firm with this maxim: "Simple, clear purpose and principles give rise to complex, intelligent behavior. Complex rules and regulations give rise to simple, stupid behavior."

In other words, command-and-control is as deadly in an organization as it is in an economy.

Humility Is Paramount for Business Success

Above all, Ulukaya values humility and character as keys to business success. Ulukaya thought maybe he should hire a CEO with more experience. He tells of interviewing "a big shot at another company, [who] had more experience as an MBA, big salary, stories written about him."

Says Ulukaya: "One day, I met him for breakfast at a diner. He was so anxious to impress me that he completely dismissed the waitress. He was really rude to her and totally disrespected her. For me, this wasn't a sign of power. It was a sign of weakness. It showed a lack of character."

The candidate for CEO "forgot what was most important," he adds. "I realized at that moment, I had more in me than I thought.

Ulukaya asked his colleagues at Chobani "what my message should be to you." Their response focused on humility. "It's great that you are a Wharton MBA. But please, don't act like it."

Ulukaya recognized that his colleagues offered wise advice: one must recognize the limits of their own mind. To the Wharton graduates, he cautioned, "Don't let [your degree] be a burden on you. Don't let it get in the way of seeing people as people and all they have to offer you, regardless of their title or position."

If we don't focus on our own character, inevitably, we will try to control others. Hock coaches us on self-management:

Humility is an essential ingredient for business success because growing a business requires examining and filtering new ideas with a sprint of discovery and openness. New ideas may invalidate old practices and deeply held beliefs.

(**Note 1**: *Epoch Times on Leadership*, "Never Forget What's Most Important: Business Advice from the CEO of Chobani, " by Barry Brownstone, January 4, 2019, page 20.)

A Leadership Essential
Delegation: The Hard Work of Letting Go
James Brooks, Joint Founder and MD, Strengths Partnership Ltd, shared his views and observations in his blog dated January 30, 2017. His thought-provoking steps to effective delegation are phenomenal lessons for leaders. As you read through the five steps, apply them,

observe the empowerment of your team and reap the rewards.

Too many leaders hang on to tasks they should be delegating and end up working long hours and feeling overwhelmed, stressed, and frustrated. They convince themselves they are indispensable, and others simply cannot do the job as expertly as they can. Deep down, these leaders simply don't want to let go. This is demoralizing, frustrating, and confusing for employees. Our experience suggests that this is one of the biggest blockers to effective leadership and positive team morale.

So how can leaders let go whilst at the same time ensuring results and standards are maintained at a high level? There are 5 steps to effective delegation:

1. Reducing limiting fears and barriers
2. Deciding what to delegate and to whom
3. Agreeing to a robust delegation process
4. Building ownership and independent thinking
5. Anticipating challenges and how to respond

Step 1: Reducing limiting fears and barriers

Effective delegation requires good awareness of yourself and your context, including a clear understanding of the fears and external barriers that get in the way of effective delegation. Typical fears/blockers we see playing out include:

Fear/Blocker	What it sounds like
Fear of failure	"If I delegate to him/her, I might fail to achieve my results."
Fear of getting upstaged	"Perhaps he/she will do the job better than me and I'll no longer be needed."

198

Lack of trust	"Don't trust anyone; if you want something done, it is better to do it yourself."
Need for control/power	"I need to ensure I control things around here otherwise nothing will get done."
Perfectionism	"Nobody can do it as well as I can."

(**Note 2**: www.strengthspartnership.com/wp-content/uploads/delegation-table.png)

Once you are more aware of your fears and blockers, you can start taking positive steps to tackle these. There is no one easy way to reduce all these barriers; however, the remaining keys should help you.

Step 2: Deciding what to delegate and to whom

Match delegated tasks to individuals on your team based on a detailed understanding of their current performance as well as what they are capable of and what energizes them. Delegate in a way that helps people to stretch positively (in other words, in areas of natural strength and energy) and progress towards their development goals.

Criteria to apply when observing and assessing people for delegation and stretch assignments include:

Aspirations - What are their career development aspirations?

Strengths - What are their natural strengths and energizers? What tasks are they passionate about?

Skills - What skills and abilities do they have?

Learning agility - How well do they learn and adapt to tasks outside their comfort zone?

Performance - What outcomes and results are they currently delivering?

Many people fail to perform delegated tasks effectively as a result of poor planning and lack of structure.

Step 3: Agreeing to a robust delegation process

There are three main areas you need to consider to ensure clarity on both what is expected and how you will remain updated and provide support. They are:

Clear goals and measures

Ensure the person knows what is expected and how this fits into the overall goals of the team and organization.

Regular check-ins

Agree on regular check-ins (this should ideally be done during regular catch-up meetings you are already having) to share progress and provide input and coaching.

Feedback and support

Provide regular, clear, and specific feedback on progress. Specify the behaviours you want to see the person use more often as well as those that should be done differently to improve results. Offer support, guidance, and coaching throughout the process to maximize the chances of success. Remember that delegation is not abdication!

Step 4: Building ownership and independent thinking

The more the individual thinks independently and takes ownership of the tasks and outcomes, the less you will need to be directly involved. There are several ways to build ownership and independent thinking including:

- Coaching
- Encouraging solutions thinking (insist on solutions, not problems)
- Ensuring people have the resources and authority to solve the problem
- Giving people space to do it their way (be tough on the 'what' or outcomes, but allow more experienced people to determine 'how'

they will go about the work)

- Showing tolerance and patience when people are learning
- Conducting regular check-ins to review progress

To understand who you should delegate to, remember that employee contribution is a function of two main variables: the person's **Performance** and the **Passion** (*energy and commitment*) they have for their work. If we plot performance on the X-axis and passion for work on the Y-axis, we can identify five different talent categories.

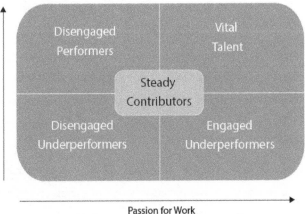

Passion for Work

Vital Talent – the star performers

Disengaged performers – the rising stars, who if engaged, will help your team to outperform

Steady performers – the "hidden heroes" who with little encouragement could raise their game and your team's results

Engaged underperformers – the toughest to manage as they are committed to the job and company, yet their performance is below the required standard

Disengaged underperformers – the most challenging team members who need help to engage with and perform their work, or to move on to something new

Step 5: Anticipating challenges and how to respond

Delegation is rarely without challenge and risk. You can easily get derailed unless you identify potential obstacles and plan for how you will deal with them.

Typical challenges include lack of alignment of expectations, lack of confidence or skill to handle the task effectively, unwillingness to ask for help, stress, and burnout, etc. I always encourage leaders to consider three different scenarios: worst case, likely case, and best case and what each might look like. This will provide you with a clearer picture of the challenges that might arise with each person when you delegate to them. Planning how to deal with these challenges means you will be prepared for the most likely challenges and can prevent them from turning into bigger problems.

> *"From what we get, we can make a living; what we give, however, makes a life."*
> Arthur Ashe

The benefits of effective delegation to you as a leader and to the business as a whole are significant in terms of increased productivity, motivation, and morale. The hardest part is letting go and overcoming your own mental barriers. By tackling some of your own fear and following the steps outlined above, it is almost certain you will become happier, healthier, and more valuable to your company.

(**Note 3**: Strengths Partnerships Ltd, "Delegation: The Hard Work of Letting Go – Leadership Essentials (Part 4)," by James Brook, Joint Founder and MD, January 30, 2017)

Fairness is Key – Put It to Practice

The new CEO of a struggling Fortune 500 company in need of a turnaround recently decided to kill a popular flexible work program, even though it boosted employee productivity and morale, reduced turnover, cut costs, and eased stress.

Marissa Mayer, you say? The 37-year-old Silicon Valley

wunderkind and new Yahoo CEO, whose decision to ban telework has been met with howls of outrage, accusations of betrayal, and endless dissection in the media?

Try Hubert Joly.

Who?

Exactly.

Welcome to what social scientists say is a common double bind for women leaders. Women are so rare in the upper echelons of power—4 percent of Fortune 500 CEOs—that their every move is closely watched, harshly judged, and often found wanting especially when it comes to how they treat other women.

Joly, the new chief executive of Best Buy, announced recently that he was ending the innovative, flexible work style the company pioneered—Results Only Work Environment, or ROWE—that defined work as something you do, not someplace you go, and gave employees control over when and where they did it.

Both Mayer's and Joly's decision were momentous steps away from the flexible work schedules that enable employees to do good work and also have lives. But we've turned the klieg lights on Marissa Mayer. Most people have never heard of Hubert Joly.

"This is one of the reasons it's so difficult to be a female executive," said Joan Williams, a law professor and director of the Center of Work Life Law at the University of California at Hastings who has been following the fallout from Mayer's decision. "Everything you do is hyper-scrutinized. And you are completely judged if you don't put a particular agenda—advancing women—incredibly high on your priority list in a way that men don't have to."

The CEO of Bank of America who made $12 million in 2012, decided recently to scale back a telework program that more than

15,000 workers in 42 states used and which, the company once boasted, save $6,000 per employee every year. The announcement which registered merely a blip on the national radar came on the heels of his decision to close the bank's popular on-site child-care-center around the country and to lay off 30,000 employees.

How about John Berry? The departing head of the Office of Personnel Management announced in March that he, too, had killed a pilot ROWE program for 400 government employees. This despite the fact that research is finding that while chance face-to-face meetings can lead to the generation of ideas—what Mayer is aiming for—bringing those ideas to life requires solitary, uninterrupted time to concentrate often far from most offices' noisy cubicle nations.

Yet Mayer has been derided as the "Stalin of Silicon Valley" and depicted by bloggers as a "Queen Bee" who has clawed her way to the top of the heap and is busily shoving other women off with her turquoise-fringed Manolos. (Yes, several articles have been written about the kind of shoes she wears, her trips to the salon for blond highlights, and her love of Oscar de la Renta.)

No one is fixated on Joly's looks. (Corporate. Gray hair. Clear-framed glasses. Needs sum.) And, unlike with Mayer, no one's called him a traitor to his sex. The truth, as Ellen Galinsky of the Families and Work Institute has found in workforce surveys, is that the people who telework and work flexibly the most are . . . *men.* While everyone's been so busy rippling on Mayer for failing to help working mothers, what's gotten lost is the fact that a growing number of working *fathers* are the ones rushing out another door to make the 6 p.m. child-care pickup. Galinsky's research has found it's not just working mothers who want flexible schedules. It's nearly 90 percent of all workers.

Yet there is no Queen Bee equivalent for a bad male boss focused on his own rise, not yours.

Imperial CEO?

Office Tyrant?

King Wasp?

(**Note 4**: *The Washington Post*, "The Business Double Standard," by Brigid Schulte, April 12, 2013, page C5.)

Understanding the Challenge Before Us

A new study released by the Senior Executives Association paints a dire picture of the federal workforce, one that is stretched too thin, hampered by old technology, and the target of partisan attacks. Without a significant overhaul, agencies may fail to provide adequate services when they are needed most, the researchers found.

The report, released in late January, seeks to answer the question in its title: "Are Declines in U.S. Federal Workforce Capabilities Putting our Government at Risk of Failing?" The conclusion of the authors, long-time government observers, and practitioners is not reassuring:

Has the U.S. federal government reached a point where critical operations might fail in stressful events that are likely to occur? This was this project's animating question. Based on the data collected in this study, it appears the answer to these critical questions is yes.

The study notes that the federal government has long-standing staffing problems in relation to increased responsibilities and a rise in overall government spending.

"The U.S. executive branch has hardly grown in 60 years. There were 1.8 million civilian employees in 1960, and 2.1 million in 2017," the study states. "Yet over the same period, the amount of money spent by the federal government has grown five-fold. To be sure, contracts and grants have filled part of the gap, but still, both the amount and range of work required of the federal workforce has continued to go up, just as the scope and complexity of executive branch functions also increased."

Compounding the challenge, several key departments have seen a brain drain from their upper echelons since President Trump's inauguration in 2017, well above the turnover seen in previous presidential transitions.

"Between 2016 and 2017, the Department of State lost 10 percent of GS-15 staff and 13 percent of the Senior Executive Service (SES); the Department of Education lost 12 percent of its GS-15 staff and 7 percent of SES; for Department of Labor 6 percent and 7 percent, for Department of Defense 7 percent and 9 percent, and for the Department of Agriculture 3 percent and 12 percent," the report found. "Another specific indicator of the turmoil was the number of GS-15s who left government but not through retirement. More than twice as many cabinet-level GS-15s quit in 2017 as in 2009, a comparable point for the previous administration."

As a result, the authors reported a trend of "increasing work overload" among federal employees, who often lack either the time or money to perform their regular duties adequately. An inadequate system for rewarding high performance coupled with "plenty of penalties" if actions don't pan out, have led to a workforce that is "fatally risk-averse and as a result, chooses inaction to action during critical times."

Perhaps most alarming has been the expansion of the number of political appointees at federal agencies over the last half-century and the deepening suspicion they seem to have of career civil servants. The study's authors found a growing desire by appointees to drive out career senior executives out of fear over their perceived personal political views, a dynamic that has ground decision-making on how to steer the federal workforce to a halt:

"Since the 1980s, executive branch leadership has been increasingly dictated by legislation and executive orders, both of which have served to politicize executive branch leadership and diminish the traditional managerial role played by career executives ... The appointees are bound to be suspicious of the civil servants because, after all, they had worked for the 'other guys' if the presidency had changed party ... In earlier years, though, the suspicion usually didn't last long: political appointees first realized that they couldn't get anything done without the civil servants, and not long after that, realized that as a general and principled rule, civil servants regarded themselves as working for the country, not any party. That seems to have changed, even dramatically. Our interlocutors spoke of dissent channels being leaked, resulting in what they regarded as 'witch hunts' ... Each change in administration is like a hostile corporate takeover. In the process, the civil service becomes demoralized and paralyzed."

To reverse course and ensure agencies can provide services to the public during potential future crises, the study recommends establishing "safe spaces" for career federal employees to focus on the non-partisan work of government, adoption of new technologies, and mitigation of vulnerabilities.

"The rapidly changing world requires new ways of organizing who does what work in public service and how to include bottom-up, more 'entrepreneurial-on-the-inside' activities not typically associated with how public service has functioned in the past," the report said.

The study also recommends a "comprehensive census for federal staffing" be done on a regular basis as part of an ongoing and systemic evaluation of government operations that need a stimulus of talent. And it argues that the private sector must take a more active role in promoting best practices, rather than simply "pursuing profits."

"If the U.S. private sector were willing to take a leadership role to help improve both local communities and the United States as a whole, in addition to pursuing profits, this too could improve the resilience of the country to future crises—after all, united we stand, divided we fall," the authors stated.

(**Note 5**: "Strengthening the Federal Workforce," by Erich Wagner, a staff correspondent at Government Executive, March 2019.)

New Trends to Consider

Acendre's federal human resource solutions and team of federal talent management experts released a whitepaper titled, "Acendre 2019 Federal Government Human Capital Trends to Watch." Based upon their research and analysis of numerous trends

> *It's better to wait and be temporarily inconvenienced than to hastily install a wrong person into a leadership position and then later have to figure out a way to remove him.*

emerging during 2019, they highlighted nine predictions that they feel would have the biggest impact on federal human resource leaders. As it relates to passing the baton, here are three that I identified as key:

Trend #4 - Big boosts for employee engagement and workforce development

The administration has stressed the importance of a high-performing workforce and wants to build a modern workforce. The envisioned modern workforce empowers senior leaders and front-line managers to align staff skills with evolving mission needs. The OPM, Office of Management and Budget (OMB), and the Defense Department are leading efforts to improve federal employee engagement, re-skill and re-deploy human capital resources to develop a simple and strategic hiring plan.

Federal News Network reports that "reskilling the existing federal workforce and improving employee engagement and performance management are still top priorities for the administration, but the change will come more in how agencies collaborate and work with one another to tackle these challenges." Furthermore, "reskilling" is also becoming an important element of agency workforce development.

Results from the annual Federal Employee Viewpoint Survey (FEVS) continue to highlight struggles agencies have in building a highly engaged workforce with strong morale. Employee engagement is becoming the newly recognized centerpiece of organizational workforce performance. While traditional thinking revolves around engagement activities for employees and employee retention, the engagement process actually begins during candidate recruitment and carries through onboarding and programs that address these points in the process are gaining attention.

The effective flow of candidates and employees carries through to the work being performed, including the learning and development of employees. Josh Bersin calls this "learning in the flow of work." Learning is evolving rapidly, including improvements so that learning is embedded into platforms where employees are working. The key driver is creating what is necessary so that learning systems can coach and train employees to improve their performance.

Ultimately, highly engaged employees are critical to establishing and maintaining a high-performing workforce. That is clearly aligned with the PMA's goals and objectives.

Trend #8 - Attention to Wellness

The benefits of healthy employees have been well documented, as have the high cost of unhealthy employees. From disengagement to stress-related injuries and sickness, not paying attention to employees' health usually has a high, negative impact.

As a May 2018 OPM memo stated, "the connection from wellness to employee engagement and productivity is well established. Both employees and agencies will benefit from reinforcing the importance of healthy living and a holistic approach to well-being through a variety of inclusive programs and services. Employers have a tremendous opportunity to help their employees see the value of adopting healthier behaviors."

With clearly defined benefits and guidance from OPM, we see agencies placing increasing importance on the health of their employees and building on their wellness programs already in place. The price for the people and agencies is too high to ignore.

Trend #9 - Collaborative work and teams

Collaboration in the workforce continues to increase because of improved technology along with evidence that collaboration and workforce teams improve workforce performance. As the federal government strives to improve performance, exploiting technology to connect employees and boost workforce performance is a logical step. Furthermore, collaboration and improved connectivity can help the workforce become more engaged, another important agency goal.

(**Note 6:** "Acendre 2019 Federal Government Human Capital Trends to Watch")

Final Thoughts

For as long as I can remember, I have watched and listened to multiple speakers on the topic of leadership espouse their views, thoughts, and insights. Their audiences were large and the diverse venues were much larger. Many of them are paid thousands of dollars by corporations, governments, academia, and churches to express their opinions in ways that captivated their audiences for an hour or two as motivational speakers, but they rarely, if ever, reference the source from which all leadership principles and strategies originate: *The Holy Bible.*

The Scriptures clearly highlight a myriad of attributes, characteristics, mannerisms, and behaviors that describe the qualities of excellent leaders. They include:

- ✓ Transparency
- ✓ Integrity
- ✓ Compassion
- ✓ Approachable
- ✓ Acumen / Intelligence
- ✓ Inspiration
- ✓ Accountability
- ✓ Service
- ✓ Respect

These, and others, were first penned in the Scriptures long before the other thousands of books were written on this topic over the generations. As you pass that baton to the next leader of your choice, refer back to chapter one and 'The Golden Rule.' I believe that it is the core of all great leaders. My personal challenge to you is to become the leader who believes in the practice of treating others in the same way that you would like to be treated. Will you accept this challenge?

STUDY QUESTIONS & DISCUSSION

1. Are you preparing any successors on your team?

_____

_____

_____

_____

_____

2. What steps are necessary to reproduce leaders to model your style?

_____

_____

_____

_____

_____

3. Is your environment conducive to learning for those who aspire to lead in your organization?

_____

_____

_____

_____

4. As you pass the baton to the next leader, how do you evaluate their progress? What feedback do you offer, if any?

_____

_____

_____

_____

_____

5. Why would leadership be attractive to those who follow you?

_____

_____

_____

_____

_____

A READER'S GUIDE:

Leadership With a Servant's Heart:
Leading Through Personal Relationships

Writing for the Lord
M I N I S T R I E S

A Conversation with Kevin Wayne Johnson

Facilitated by Mr. Dave Farrow

Farrow Communications

Brain Hacker series – www.brainhackers.com

1-866-949-6868

Buffalo, New York (USA)

Published on April 17, 2019

"What Makes A Great Leader" – episode 191

https://www.youtube.com/watch?v=giKhH4fqpZs

The Interview

Mr. Dave Farrow is twice listed in the Guinness Book of World Records for Greatest Memory. He is a fun and impactful speaker whose program, *The Farrow Method*, an international bestseller has proven effective in a double-blind neuroscience study at McGill University. He is the CEO of a successful marketing firm and training business, a digital magazine, and he is the host of the YouTube and Podcast series *The Brains Behind It. The Farrow Brain Games* is an internationally recognized mental sport played worldwide. Farrow has been featured on over 2,000 media interviews, and *The Farrow Memory Program* spent over a year on the Amazon bestseller list in the category of memory, leading to a sponsorship deal with SONY and two venture-backed infomercials resulting in estimated sales of over $10 Million worldwide.

MR. FARROW: Hey there, Brainhackers, Dave Farrow here. I'm talking with Kevin Wayne Johnson about this upcoming incredible shift happening generationally in society today. He says that because of this generational shift we are losing all of our leadership in these great institutions and that it could have repercussions in every aspect of society. So if you are a leader, if you are the younger generation, and you want to figure out how to fulfill that role and step into your destiny, then come listen to us right after this. Hey, Kevin. Welcome to the show.

MR. JOHNSON: Hey, there. How are you today?

MR. FARROW: I'm doing good. So you are a best-selling author. And your topic, you do a lot of coaching and consulting, really around leadership. And you specifically have this incredible dire warning about the leadership of institutions. So we're talking governmental, religious, business, private sector, everything. You're saying that because baby boomers are retiring, because a whole strata of leadership for so long is retiring and going away, that we're going to face a real crisis of identity. Is that the idea?

MR. JOHNSON: You hit it right on the head. And you said "going to retire," but I would fast forward and say have retired. Those of us that were born between 1946 and 1964—I mean, there were millions of us—and we've gone through our careers now, and we've left behind a group of current and next-generation leaders that really need our help in terms of coaching and mentoring. But most of us have left.

MR. FARROW: So what about this where somebody is like a twenty-something right now. What if they say, 'Oh, good riddance. You guys are part of an old generation. You have old ideas and I'm all into this new stuff and you guys are really out of touch.' Isn't this just kind of the same topic we hear generation after generation: that the young replaces the old? And there are always these warnings that we're missing out on something, but maybe you know the younger generation just does it differently.

MR. JOHNSON: No, not at all. Not at all. And the reason is because great leadership practices, and principles, and strategies are core to who we are as human beings. How do we go about caring for people, how we value people –

MR. FARROW: We're timeless.

MR. JOHNSON: – how we treat people, how they add value, and we tell them that we appreciate them. That's the core tenet of what leadership is all about. And it has to be taught; it has to be transferred. People have to actually see it in action. So the warning has more to do with the fact that there are fewer, and fewer, and fewer of us from the baby boom generation in the workplace right now than there were five, ten years ago. And the big concern is, who's going to reach back and actually help the current generation to be the great leaders that we know they can be. But we have to be taught. You're not necessarily born with these skills; you have to learn these strategies and principles in order to implement and execute.

MR. FARROW: I have what you're saying. I'm part of Gen X, so I'm kind of sandwiched in the middle. You know, there's this big battle, I guess, between the baby boomers and the millennials, and I feel like I'm just . . . I don't know. I love the grunge era; I'm all a 90s brat. Who knows. I'm kind of stuck in the middle there. But yeah, even me—I'm looking towards retiring. That's obviously very early for myself. But, you know, I'm looking at that in my life at some point. And everybody who works for me, they're all millennial types. And I try to pass on as much as I can, but there's also a lot that they show me, and they do things a little differently. But sometimes it's even better and more innovative.

MR. JOHNSON: Yeah.

MR. FARROW: So do you find that this is like you are preaching down to them saying, 'Hey, you got to listen to me; there's something you're missing'? Do you think they're doing it wrong?

MR. JOHNSON: No.

MR. FARROW: Or is it just . . . is this something that you're getting from them? It's like, you have a whole bunch of people who are the younger generation saying, 'Hey, we need this; we're missing out on this,' and you think that older folks have to step up?

MR. JOHNSON: Yeah, I would say it's the latter. I've never preached down at anyone because we're always working collaboratively and in cooperation to make sure that the workplace is as best as it can be and that these organizations are attractive and not a repellent. And what I mean by that is, the better trained the workforce and the better the leadership within that particular organization, they become a magnet and more people want to come work with them. So we do this together. This is collaborative and cooperative because we want to hear the ideas from the questions that are coming forth. Prior to my retirement, when I was mentoring and coaching, I was getting a lot of questions from the future leaders—the folks who I passed the baton to. And they're still asking the question. So my job is to avail myself to help them to be better communicators, to help them to recognize that we manage things, but we lead people. There is a difference. We don't manage people; we manage things. But we lead the people and all of the dynamics that are involved with that.

MR. FARROW: That's great. That reminds me of a phrase.

Something along [the] lines of, you use things and work with people, never the other way around.

MR. JOHNSON: Right.

MR. FARROW: Never use people and work with things.

MR. JOHNSON: Exactly.

MR. FARROW: Okay. So let's get down to the brass tacks. How do we actually do this? What do you think, let's say a bigger organization needs to do in order to actually try to mentor the next generation without being preachy, without talking down to them, without trying to replace them, without trying to make a clone of themselves, and actually let them have some autonomy? What do we need to do to reach them?

MR. JOHNSON: Well, some of the things that we can do together as we work together as a part of our training is, we do a lot of facilitating and a lot of classroom exercises. We have open dialogue, open discussion, open conversations, so we can teach each other the principles of listening and communication. You and I are having a conversation right now, and there are a number of people watching all around the world. But if we're not connecting, then we're not effectively communicating. And that has to do with leadership. Also, how do we go about influencing people? Not necessarily from our position but based upon the type of person we are, the leader we are. So we have a responsibility to make sure that we value people, that everyone feels like they're a contribution to the team, that they have something to add. And some of the basic things that people can do is just to make sure that we hear each other out, to make sure that their input and their feedback is heard, even if it's not received and executed and implemented. At least we'd want to be able to hear them out. And then making sure that as leaders we're always growing ourselves so that we can grow our team and ultimately grow our organization. So all of those different mechanics and principles of strategies are sort of going on at the same time. And again, we're not born knowing this information; it has to be taught.

MR. FARROW: Yeah.

MR. JOHNSON: So those are just some of the things that we can do as leaders; those of us that have moved on and are now reaching back to do the training and development, that's what we do. But like I said earlier: we do it together, not as one on a pedestal looking down.

MR. FARROW: Now, how is this done in a practical sense? Is this like you suggest that people need to volunteer with their local organizations? I know you do this for a fee where you go into organizations and do leadership development training. I know a lot of people that do that as well. But is this something you suggest people volunteer to do, or is this something that they need to do in their own organizations and take a larger role in the community, or what?

MR. JOHNSON: Well, it's a combination of both. I mean, everyone is really not interested necessarily in being a leader, or a manager, or a supervisor. So no one should be forced. But the reality is, a lot of people do a really, really great job at what they do in their career field. They become subject matter experts. And then their bosses determined, uh, you need to be a leader now because you're really good at what you do. They may be a subject matter expert, but they don't necessarily know how to lead people. And that's where we step in and help.

MR. FARROW: Oh, the Peter Principle.

MR. JOHNSON: It's voluntary. You know, you don't make a person become a leader. But a lot of our leaders end up in these positions because they're experts in what they do. They have the knowledge. And so we come alongside them and just kind of give them that help. But, no, we never recommend forcing anyone to become a supervisor, or to be [a] manager, or a leader because there's a lot of responsibility involved in it.

MR. FARROW: What you're talking about is the Peter Principle, that principle that states that most people who are in management positions are incompetent because they were really good at the position that was slightly below them, and they were so good they were promoted. And people are always promoted slightly one level above their own competence level. So let's say I'm really good at sales. I hit these sales records over and over, then I'm put in charge of the sales team. But the problem is, I might not be a very good manager. I might suck at managing, but I might be great at sales. So, you know, that sort of thing happens a lot. So you really think it's a training issue—that people just need a little bit of training in order to become a leader because inevitably if they're competent at something, they're going to find themselves in that position where they are passing on their knowledge.

MR. JOHNSON: Yeah, absolutely. And there's no doubt that the potential is there for them to be a great manager and to be a great leader. But with the right grooming, and the right instruction, and the right training, and the right mentorship, and the right coaching, they would be even much better. Think about this for a minute. Think about these athletes. My family and I have a wonderful opportunity to go to the Summer Olympics every four years. And we've been going to the Olympics in Atlanta since 1996. And I get a chance to watch these world-class athletes represent their countries from all over the world. How did they become a world-class athlete? Through the training.

MR. FARROW: A lot of sacrifice and commitment, a lot of

training, and obviously a certain amount of genetic predisposition and talent too.

MR. JOHNSON: Absolutely. So it is in the workplace. We have great potential of young men and young women in the workplace today, in our churches and our nonprofit organizations, in our government agencies—all across the United States and the world. But they need the ongoing training, and coaching, and mentoring to be the best leader in what they're doing. And that's the analogy that we draw.

MR. FARROW: All right. So I'm a big believer in mentoring. How does somebody go about this? If I wanted to mentor people what would you suggest in that situation?

MR. JOHNSON: Well, I would suggest the same thing that I did. When I was a young pup in the workplace I would look to different men and women that were there that just had that look and thus carried themselves in a very professional way. And I would just reach out to them and say, 'Look, I would very much like to get to your level one day; don't know how long it would take, but would you help me and show me some of the tips to get there? Would you mentor me?' And more times than not they would say yes. Very few people in my career ever said no. Some did, but very few.

MR. FARROW: But that's somebody you're asking. What about on the mentor side? What's a way a mentor can try to help somebody? Should you look for people who are maybe floundering or disorganized at work and say, can I give you some advice? That's probably the more dangerous situation.

MR. JOHNSON: Yeah.

MR. FARROW: Because it can be construed as very offensive if you just out and out try to mentor somebody [without their permission] to help them out even if you have good intentions.

MR. JOHNSON: Yeah, yeah. We think alike. You're right. Those good intentions could go awry. So a number of organizations nowadays have what they call a volunteer system where they have different leaders in the different organizations that are willing to avail themselves to serve as a mentor. And those younger individuals within the organizations are looking for a mentor. And they'll just sign up and they'll get assigned that way, and the two will work together to make the relationship work well. The mentor would feed into the life of the mentee and kind of help them along the way. One thing that I do recommend and that's worked out really, really well for me and many, many others in the workplace, is to have a mentor that doesn't look like you and a mentor that's not in your career field, and have them to feed some good information into your life because you don't necessarily want an architect to an architect. Why not have a registered nurse mentor a car mechanic?

MR. FARROW: Well, now that's interesting. That kind of goes counter to specialization. A lot of people think they do need that: if they want to get ahead in architecture, they get an architect. You know?

MR. JOHNSON: Right. Yeah, I mean, they could. But the more diverse the team is that helps us to get to the next place, you're going to start to find out that you have a diversity of thought, you're able to see things through a different lens, and you're actually able to think much differently than you would. You'll think outside of your box when it comes to solving problems and making decisions. And so that architect to architect, they think alike. And that's okay.

MR. FARROW: You know, actually, I would add one extra layer to that. I would add politics. I think there are a lot of people who look very, very different but think so alike. Yet it seems politics is the last final frontier of tribalism, you know? And I have a lot of very, very liberal friends, for example, that really benefited from having somebody who is very conservative in their life. And I'm not talking necessarily like they voted conservative or republican each time. I think there's a difference in Republican and conservative for that matter. But you have somebody talking about the role of the state and other people talking about the role of charities and the family. It's like kind of a counterpoint to some of the assumptions that we make, especially if you grew up with some very, very hard-felt assumptions, you know?

MR. JOHNSON: Right.

MR. FARROW: Having those things challenged, seeing them from a different perspective, can be very, very enlightening.

MR. JOHNSON: Yeah, yeah. I totally agree. Again, it helps us all to see this world through a different lens. And it also helps us to take a look at things from a different perspective. And it makes us a much more well-rounded person. So that's why I recommend that you look for someone who doesn't look like you and who is not even in your career field.

MR. FARROW: I agree with that.

MR. JOHNSON: Because they're going to help you think outside of your box.

MR. FARROW: You know, I actually had some of the greatest impact in my life, in terms of my thought process recently. It came from a really good friend of mine, Sergio Gonzales, over at eBay. He's no longer working at eBay, but he's very much connected to the whole Bay Area and the Silicon Valley scene. And the conversations we would have are just absolutely fascinating . . . kind of in that Silicon Valley way of disruption and it gets rid of all of your preconceived notions. I actually have to start over. And I would talk about a a business model that we're doing. And he goes, 'Well, why are you doing that? Really, no. Why are you doing that? Well, why are you doing that? What if all that's not going to work out? What are you going to do instead? And he'd go on: What if that's really the completely wrong thing that you should do and you should be doing something totally different?' He'd be just asking those questions that in any other context I think would be incredibly offensive; but from him it's disruptive.

MR. JOHNSON: Yeah.

MR. FARROW: And that sort of disruptive perspective was exactly what I needed during those times.

MR. JOHNSON: Now, you made a great point. So part of what he did in having those sessions with you is an extension of leadership. In this particular example, he knew how to set the tone, and set the environment and the atmosphere so that when you entered into this relationship no one would be offended because you sort of understood the boundaries. That's part of the art.

MR. FARROW: I tried very hard to never be offended by anything.

MR. JOHNSON: Yeah.

MR. FARROW: I find it really difficult to find offense in it. I usually think if I'm offended by somebody's actions, that's my failing not theirs. That's the way I see it.

MR. JOHNSON: Exactly. A good leader has to be aware of that, and everyone is not aware of that. And everybody doesn't echo what you just said.

MR. FARROW: Yeah, good point.

MR. JOHNSON: And that's a very important principle. Because of the society in which we live right now, where there's a lot of angst, there's a lot of anger, social media, technology, etcetera, etcetera, people are on edge a lot more today than they were five, ten years ago.

MR. FARROW: True.

MR. JOHNSON: And we have to be careful with how we handle people. We really do. That's just the reality of where we are.

MR. FARROW: No. That makes a lot of sense. So being careful and conscientious of that is really important, and that's all right. Well, I think there are some great ideas that you brought up. If you're a young person that wants to get involved in something and you want to get a mentor, then finding people from different backgrounds with different perspectives is really important. Maybe also finding somebody in your field, but maybe that field is not right for you and you should think of somebody who challenges your thoughts. Work on not being offended by things. Work on opening your mind up. And like Bruce Lee used to say, you empty your cup so that it can be filled. You know, if you already think you know everything, you can't learn anything, and you can't really grow as a human being.

MR. JOHNSON: Right.

MR. FARROW: That's a terrible place to be.

MR. JOHNSON: Right.

MR. FARROW: So open up your mind to that. Any other final tips for any individual, for any young people out there? You know, I would also say that it's very, very difficult for young men to find mentors nowadays. And I find that a lot of men learn a lot from mentoring, I think, and that is not to play gender roles or anything, but traditionally, women have a larger group of people to have sounding boards around them. And I really find a lot of men are isolating themselves lately and it's really dangerous. What would you say to them on how to find a mentor that can really bring them out of that shell and help make them the best they can be?

MR. JOHNSON: Well, again, not for the sake of repeating myself, but I want to echo it again: When you see someone in your life that you kind of model, you sort of emulate the way they present themselves, and you say to yourself, I think I would like to have a conversation with this person. Don't hesitate to approach them and ask them the question. You'll be surprised more times than not, because people are honored to do it. Now, mentoring can also go the other way around. In our current and next generation of leaders, there are some outstanding and brilliant minds out there who can also mentor those of us that are chronologically older in age, especially as we move into a new career field, or we do something different now that we're in retirement. So it's not always the older person mentoring the young person. Sometimes it's the younger person who's absolutely brilliant, mentoring the older person that's trying to catch up and stay ahead.

MR. FARROW: Actually, my example of Silicon Valley was very much like that, although I don't know . . . I don't really know if Sergio is older or younger than me, but it definitely was that kind of younger vibe of disruption that made me rethink some of my preconceived notions. So it goes both ways.

MR. JOHNSON: Yeah.

MR. FARROW: I can't really improve on that. That's a great way to end our interview. Thank you very much for being on the show.

MR. JOHNSON: All right. Thank you.

Listen to Your Heart

If you can live
the life that you believe in
you will have everything you need
to reach your dream.

Just look into your heart
and you'll find confidence in yourself
that will make each challenge
easier to face…

You'll discover the hope
that will keep you believing…
you'll find an inner strength
that will help you past obstacles…
and you'll see the happiness
that's waiting for you
if you keep trying…

The struggle for any dream
is always worth the effort,
for in the struggle lies its
strength and fulfillment…

If you listen to your heart
you will reach your dream.

Larry S. Chengges
©1986 by Springbrook Publications, Inc.

Reading Group Questions & Topics for Discussion

1. Describe your leadership strengths and how you will continually build upon these strengths to improve your influence with others.

_____

_____

_____

_____

_____

2. How do you navigate your team through turbulent times and challenges?

_____

_____

_____

_____

_____

3. What are the top three characteristics that describe your leadership style? Why did you select these as your top three?

_____

_____

_____

4. If given the task of establishing a new organization, what qualities are you looking for in your leadership team?

_____

_____

_____

_____

_____

5. How do you maintain your energy and drive to achieve excellence? Give two specific examples.

_____

_____

_____

_____

_____

6. Is it possible to re-engage with a person on your team who has disengaged? If so, describe the process that would lead to success.

_____

_____

_____

_____

_____

7. Change is difficult for most people but is necessary to move an organization forward. How do you handle change and lead others to accept it?

_____

_____

_____

_____

_____

8. What is the significance of Philippians 2:4 as it pertains to leaders?

_____

_____

_____

_____

_____

9. In light of the current climate in your country, what transformational leadership skills are needed most?

_____

_____

_____

_____

_____

10. As a leader, what five persons do you presently mentor?

_____

_____

_____

_____

11. Different personality types can be the precursor for conflict in the workplace. Name some strategies that you would utilize to ease the tensions.

_____

_____

_____

_____

_____

12. How would you motivate a negative person on your team to improve their performance?

_____

_____

_____

_____

_____

13. Share the moment in your life when you realized that many followers were counting upon your leadership. Did you feel prepared for the challenge? Why or why not?

_____

_____

_____

_____

_____

14. What leader had the most profound influence in your life? How?

_____

_____

_____

_____

_____

15. Name the key differences between coaching and mentoring.

_____

_____

_____

_____

_____

16. Leadership is not necessarily positional. In what three ways can you influence positive change in your organization regardless of your current position?

_____

_____

_____

_____

_____

17. Leadership is about service to others. Is 'service' a key aspect of your day-to-day interactions with others?

_____

_____

_____

_____

18. In his book titled *21 Laws of Leadership in the Bible: Learning to Lead from the Men and Women of Scripture,* John C. Maxwell shares relevant principles that are time-tested and centuries old. Which appeals to you most and why?

_____

_____

_____

_____

_____

19. The need for good leaders has reached a critical point. How do you identify candidates for key leadership positions in your organization?

_____

_____

_____

_____

_____

20. Will an organization meet its stated objectives with 'bad' leadership? Explain.

_____

_____

_____

_____

_____

21. Name leadership strategies that you would use to motivate a change of behavior with an under-performing member of your team.

_____

_____

_____

_____

_____

Selected Bibliography & Recommended Reading

10 Leadership Maneuvers: A General's Guide to Serving and Leading, by Loren Reno, Deep River Books, ©2015.

21 Laws of Leadership in the Bible: Learning to Lead from the Men and Women of Scripture, by John C. Maxwell, Thomas Nelson, ©2007.

21 Qualities of Leaders in the Bible: Developing Leadership Traits Inspired by the Men and Women of Scripture, by John C. Maxwell, Thomas Nelson, ©2019.

A Goal is a Dream with a Deadline: Extraordinary Wisdom for Entrepreneurs, Managers and Other Smart People, by Leo B. Helzel and Friends, McGraw Hill, Inc., ©1995.

"Acendre 2019 Federal Government Human Capital Trends to Watch," Talent Management Solutions

Becoming the Best: Build a World-Class Organization through Values-Based Leadership, by Harry M. Jansen Kraemer, Jr. John Wiley & Sons, ©2015.

Crossing the Finish Line: Getting to the Top and Staying There, by Addie Perkins Williamson, Ph.D., Lulu Publishing Services, ©2013.

Dare to Lead: Brave Work, Tough Conversations, Whole Hearts, by Brene Brown, Random House, ©2018.

Dare to Succeed: A Treasury of Inspiration and Wisdom for Life and Career, presented by Van Couch Communications, Honor Books, ©1994.

Developing the Leaders Around You: How to Help Others Reach Their Potential, by John C. Maxwell, Thomas Nelson Publishers, ©1995.

Faith: 90 Devotions for OUR DAILY BREAD, compiled by Dave Branon, Our Daily Bread Ministries, ©2016.

First Things First: To Live, to Love, to Learn, to Leave a Legacy, by Stephen R. Covey, Simon and Schuster, ©1994.

"Free Thinkers Leader's Guide to the Real World," by Ashley Goodall, *Harvard Business Review,* April 2019.

Good to Great: Why Some Companies Make the Leap...and Others Don't, by Jim Collins, Harper Business, ©2001.

Great Jobs for Everyone 50+: Finding Work that Keeps You Happy and Healthy...and Pays the Bills, by Kerry Hannon, Wiley Global Finance (for AARP), ©2012.

How to Reach Your Life Goals, by Peter J. Daniels, The House of Tabor, ©1985.

If You Can See it – You Can Be It: 12 Street Smart Recipes for Success, by Chef Jeff Henderson, Smiley Books, ©2013.

Inside the Five-Sided Box: Lessons from a Lifetime of Leadership in the Pentagon, by Ash Carter, Penguin, ©2019.

Insights on Successful Leadership: Helpful Advice for Those Who are Leaders and For Those Who Long to Become Leaders, by Rick Renner, Teach All Nations, ©2004.

Jack Welch and the GE Way: Management Insights and Leadership Secrets of the Legendary CEO, by Roger Slater, McGraw Hill, ©1999.

Leaders Eat Last: Why Some Teams Pull Together and Others Don't, by Simon Sinek, Penguin Group, ©2014.

Leaders that Last: How Covenant Friendships Can Help Pastors Thrive, by Gary D. Kinnaman and Alfred H. Ellis, Baker Books, ©2003.

Leveraged Learning: How the Disruption of Education Helps Lifelong Learners and Experts with Something to Teach, by Danny Iny, IdeaPress Publishing, ©2018.

Jesus CEO: Using Ancient Wisdom for Visionary Leadership, by Laurie Beth Jones, Hyperion, ©1995.

"Nine Lies about Work: Freethinking Leader's Guide to the Real World," by Marcus Buckingham and Ashley Goodall, *Harvard Business Review* Press

Principle-Centered Leadership, by Stephen R. Covey, Simon and Schuster, ©1990.

Quiet Strength: The Principles, Practices, and Priorities of a Winning Life, by Tony Dungy_and Nathan Whitaker, Tyndale House Publishers, ©2008.

Seeing the BIG Picture: Business Acumen to Build Your Credibility, Career and Company, by Kevin Cope, Greenleaf Book Group Press, ©2012.

S.H.A.P.E.: Finding and Fulfilling Your Unique Purpose for Life, by Eric Rees, Zondervan, ©2006.

Strengthening the Federal Workforce: The Civil Service is at a Crossroads, by Erich Wagner, Donald F. Kettl, Paul Verkuil, Howard Risher & John Kamensky, March 2019, Government Executive.

Strengths Finder 2.0, by Tom Rath, Gallup Press, ©2007.

Switch: How to Change Things when Change is Hard, by Chip Heath and Dan Heath, Broadway Books, ©2010.

The Coaching Habit: Say Less, Ask More & Change the Way You Lead Forever, by Michael Bungay Stanier, Box of Crayons Press, ©2016.

The Empowered Mind: How to Harness the Creative Force Within You, by Gini Graham Scott, Prentice Hall, ©1994.

The 15 Invaluable Laws of Growth: Live Them and Reach Your Potential, by John C. Maxwell, Center Street, ©2012.

The Heart of a Leader: Insights on the Art of Influence, by Ken Blanchard, Honor Books, ©1999.

The High-Definition Leader: Building Multi-Ethnic Churches in a Multi-Ethnic World, by Derwin L. Gray, Thomas Nelson, ©2015.

The Holy Spirit: His Gifts and Power Are For You, by Dr. Eugene G. Givens, Books of Value, ©2011.

The Leadership Wisdom of Solomon: 28 Essential Strategies for Leading and Integrity, by Pat Williams with Jim Denney, Standard Publishing, ©2010.

The Outward Mindset: Seeing Beyond Ourselves (How to Change Lives & Transform Organizations), by The Arbinger Institute, Berrett-Koehler Publishers, Inc., ©2016.

The 108 Skills of Natural Born Leaders, by Warren Blank, AMACON, ©2001.

The Power of Choice: Embracing Efficacy to Drive Your Career, by Michael C. Hyter, Global Novations, LLC, ©2011.

The 7 Powers of Questions: Secrets to Successful Communication in Life and at Work, by Dorothy Leeds, The Berkeley Publishing Group, ©2000.

The Transformation Challenge: The Six-Steps to Planning and Execution, by Steven and Robert Shallenberger, Becoming Your Best Global Leadership, ©2017

Understanding Your Potential: Discover the Hidden You, by Dr. Myles Munroe, Destiny Image Publishers, ©1991.

You Cannot Afford the Luxury of a Negative Thought: A Book for People with Any Life-Threatening Illness-Including Life, The Life 101 Series, by John-Roger and Peter McWilliams, Prelude Press, ©1991.

Who Moved My Cheese? by Spencer Johnson, M.D., G. P. Putnam's Sons, ©1998.

Why Do So Many Incompetent Men Become Leaders? (And How to Fix It), by Tomas Chamorro-Premuzic, Harvard Business Review Press, March 2019.

Why Motivating People Doesn't Work and What Does: The New Science of Leading, Energizing and Engaging, by Susan Fowler, Berrett-Koehler Publishers, Inc., ©2014.

About the Author

Because he says, *"God uses ordinary people to accomplish extraordinary things,"* **Kevin Wayne Johnson** has taken up the task of developing individual and organizational operating excellence as his life's ministry. He coaches to coax audiences to live out their gifts, and in the words of his national best-selling book series, to then *"Give God the Glory!"* This book series has earned the current radio and television host some 19 literary awards, since 2001. Gayle King, an editor-at-large for O, The Oprah Magazine, praised his work, writing to him that *"Your book, Kevin, touched me."*

Johnson is the Founder, Chief Visionary and CEO of The Johnson Leadership Group, LLC, and is an independent certified coach, teacher, and speaker with the nationally recognized John Maxwell Team, where he leads learning experiences tailored to meet the specific needs of the audience to help maximize efficiency, growth, awareness, and effectiveness. Johnson provides organizations and the people who work within them with the tools to forge effective personal and interpersonal communication. He delivers training on the elements of dynamic relationships to equip teams with the attitudes and attributes needed to develop individuals into leaders. He does so through motivating workshops, seminars, insightful keynote speeches, and compassionate coaching—all to encourage personal and professional growth.

Johnson enjoyed a 34-year career (*retired*) in government and private industry as a middle-to-senior level leader. He has managed and led workforce development, executive training, organizational change, acquisition/procurement, customer service, client relationships, security, records management, property administration, facilities, and human resources. He was a key leader on the National Performance Review for Procurement and Customer Service Reform, under the Clinton Administration from 1993-1996, has testified before the U.S. House of Representatives Small Business Committee on Procurement Reform, and has prepared written testimony for the District of Columbia Committee on Government Operations.

A native of Richmond, Virginia, Johnson earned a B.S. in Business Administration and Management / Economics / Finance from Virginia Commonwealth University and completed coursework towards an M.B.A. at Marymount University and the University of Colorado at Colorado Springs. He is also a graduate of the True Disciple Ministries Bible Institute, Somerville, New Jersey. He is an ordained Church of God minister who has served in multiple leadership positions at the local, regional, national, and international levels over the past twenty years, including Senior Pastor. He currently serves as the Faith Community Commissioner—Maryland Governor's Commission for Suicide Commission and is on the National Board of Directors of Nexus Youth and Family Solutions.

He lives in Clarksville, Maryland, with his wife Gail of twenty-six years and their three sons: Kevin, Christopher, and Cameron.

International Coach Federation

About the Author (Foreword)

The foreword for this book was written by **Mr. Ed DeCosta**. Ed is a senior member of The John Maxwell Team as a well-traveled speaker, trainer, coach, and mentor.

Ed DeCosta is one of the most engaging executive coaches of our time. Whether working with entrepreneurial companies or Fortune 500 corporations, he delivers results. He's a global speaker who has shared the stage with the likes of John C. Maxwell, Darren Hardy, Les Brown, Nick Vujicic, and more. He is an acclaimed author whose books include *ASCEND* and *Release Your Superhero*. His full bio can be viewed at: www.eddecosta.com.

Ed has changed countless lives as the developer and publisher of the global online personal development training program *Ascend on Demand*. He's a force on social media with hundreds of thousands of followers on Twitter, Facebook, LinkedIn, and Instagram. Ed is the host of a long-standing weekly coaching blog and is also the star of the weekly YouTube show "Get Edified," with thousands of followers.

BOOK

Pastor Kevin Wayne Johnson

Life-Changing Keynote Speaker
Certified John Maxwell Coach/Trainer
Workshop Presenter and Award-winning Author

CONFERENCES
Leadership Training, Writing/Publishing Seminars

WORKSHOPS
Professional Development Presentations & MORE!

FOR MORE INFORMATION & BOOKING CALL
(410) 340-8633

facebook@KevinWayneJohnsonPage
twitter@writing4thelord

www.KevinWayneJohnson.com

*"If any man speak, let him speak as the oracles of God:
if any man minister, let him do it as of the ability which
God giveth: that God in all things may be glorified
through Jesus Christ, to whom be praise and
dominion for ever and ever. Amen."*
1 Peter 4:11

Kevin Wayne Johnson is available to speak and share his proven *servant* leadership principles and strategies at your next event as well as coach and mentor your workforce...Book today!!

Listen to Kevin Wayne Johnson's on-air broadcast, as co-host, reaching the local, regional, national, and international markets monthly.

The **JOHNSON**
LEADERSHIP GROUP
Certified Leadership Expert
(Mentor, Coach, Trainer and Speaker)

As Founder and Chief Executive of **The Johnson Leadership Group**, Kevin provides organizations and the people who work within them with the tools to forge effective personnel and interpersonal communication. He delivers training on the elements of dynamic relationships to equip teams with the attitudes and attributes needed to develop individuals into leaders. He does so through motivating workshops, seminars, insightful keynote speeches, and compassionate coaching—all to encourage personal and professional growth. He is a John Maxwell Team certified trainer, coach, mentor, and speaker.

Mission: To equip the current and next generation of leaders to achieve greatness.

Vision: Creating leaders of excellence at all levels.

Five (5) Strategic Goals:

1. Deliver on-time and best-in-class leadership development principles and strategies.

2. Improve our clients' communication channels that lead to informed decisions for the workforce.

3. Promote better informed decisions amongst our client's leadership team(s).

4. Strengthen organizational excellence, accountability, and stewardship.

5. Measure and monitor performance goals for the clients quarterly.

Website: www.TheJohnsonLeadershipGroup.com

We facilitate training, coaching, and mentor for front-line, mid-level, and senior-level staff in government agencies, corporations, non-profit organizations, churches, and academia.

To order additional copies

of this book or others:

www.amazon.com

@kevinwaynejohnson

www.TheJohnsonLeadershipGroup.com

The **JOHNSON**
LEADERSHIP GROUP
Certified Leadership Expert
(Mentor, Coach, Trainer and Speaker)

www.KevinWayneJohnson.com

KEVINWAYNEJOHNSON

CPSIA information can be obtained
at www.ICGtesting.com
Printed in the USA
LVHW091342100320
649570LV00002BA/38